Bullies Among Us

A "Simple" Guide to Stop Bullying at School and at Work

By Michael Shawn Keller

This is a work of nonfiction. The events and experiences detailed herein are all true. Some names, identities, and circumstances have been changed in order to protect the privacy and/or anonymity of the various individuals involved.

The information in this book is not intended to replace the services of a qualified professional. If you know or suspect that you have a particular problem described in this book, you should consult a professional.

In an effort to be gender neutral, the author has randomly interspersed male and female pronouns when the gender of the noun is not known.

ISBN-13: 978-0692728734

ISBN-10: 0692728732

Printed in the United States of America

www.lifeinaweek.com

www.bulliesamongus.com

This book is dedicated to anyone who is dealing with or has dealt with bullying in his life.

Growing Up Bullied

by Chris Nastu, Sr.

When I was young it was tough to be that age.

Ten years old and a sixteen-year old trying to drown me daily.

But my parents did not believe.

As I was dunked and held under water time and time again.

Go home to mama, and not to be believed ever or ever.

Kept in a dog house for the entire day

Or he would tell my parents that I enjoyed cigarettes.

Beaten and beaten again.

But my parents could I tell them, when?

Never because I was the one that was wrong

Not the bully trying to kill me with sand

Down my throat and in my ears, let them see

The way I was treated. They would never see.

As I went to bed as no one believed

The room closed in every night like a sleeve

Squeezing and squashing my chest so tight.

Would I be able to survive another night?

The room closing in and my body so thick

Seeing pots and pans flying off of the shelves.

Can't you help me from bullies like this?

No one would and It seemed so a bliss,

That I always had to feel like this.

Table of Contents

Bullies Among Us

A "Simple" Guide to Stop Bullying at School and at Work

Part One: Bullying at School

What is Bullying?

Overcoming bullying is challenging, to be sure. Before we begin to fully understand a definition of bullying that will help us to overcome this challenge, we must first dispel some popular misconceptions about bullying, misconceptions that would thwart our progress towards eliminating it. What I want to accomplish in this section is to break down our general ideas of bullying—even if we believe them to be correct—and then rebuild our conceptions of bullying from the beginning. We will also see where some of our old ideas have come from and how to go about changing them.

I could have told you that bullying was habitually beating others who are weaker. While this is how the dictionary and even schools have described it in the past, I don't believe this is a very practical definition, as you will go on to discover too. I want you to know the real truth behind bullying. Once we understand this, we can deal with it better.

A popular misconception is that bullying is an uncontrollable factor. It usually takes place behind locked doors in locker rooms, at dance recitals or just before lunchtime. This is not entirely true. While bullying does occur in these places and in these ways, these are far from the only circumstances. Bullying is everywhere. Media images such as Nelson Muntz from *The Simpsons* show, holding other kids against the wall to take their lunch money, spring to mind. Three factors here are wrong with these beliefs. Can you guess what they are?

The first is that bullying is not always physical. The popular cliché of "sticks and stones will break my bones, but words will never hurt me" is simply a fallacy. Words do hurt! In fact, they are very powerful tools of attack and a popular selection of actions that bullies can take.

The second is that bullying does not just take place in private. It can take place virtually anywhere children or adults gather. Additionally, and especially with the rise in technology in recent times, bullying can even occur online, as you will later read about.

The third stereotype of bullies is that they are just children. While bullying is most common during younger years, there is not a specific age in which it stops entirely. In fact, it may occur well into adulthood, as we will learn about in chapter two.

One of the more realistic movies I've seen about bullying is called Mean Girls. It is about a group of popular girls who hold the philosophy that they are better than everyone else. Not having social acceptance into this group can be emotionally challenging enough, but they build a reputation up at the school which gives them an honored authority and their feedback is respected. While the film is much closer to developing an accurate portrayal of bullying—with its notorious Hollywood twists—there are several flaws.

Bullying may often be materialistic in the sense of not wearing the right brands, displaying the right authentic logos, or being what others consider pretty or cool. However, in the film, Mean Girls, the school did not have aggressive policies to prevent the characters from basically running the school. In reality, today there are policies at most schools to help prevent harassment and many schools express their dedication towards eliminating any bullying in all its forms.

Years ago, popular media almost always portrayed a dead end approach to bullying, where characters often fell victim to bullies with no way out. Luckily, today bullying is all over the news and the spotlight is finally helping to put an end to its vicious cycle.

Bullying is not a dead end. In many aspects of life aside from bullying, many people feel they are stuck at dead ends simply because they don't know how to solve the problems they are facing. They may see indications of a dead end and simply give up without resistance. This goes for all aspects of life, whether it is a dead end job, a relationship that you feel you just settled for and aren't happy with, a friend or co-worker that is constantly putting you down, or anything that seems hopeless. But you are not stuck. You can change your situation; you can change your life, and I hope to help you with that.

One of the most important things I do in my life is to surround myself with people of honest character and good-hearted spirit; people who are goal-oriented to constantly better themselves. I recall a speech given by Eddie Johnson, an amazing basketball player and person. The two things from his speech that stuck with me were, "always try to be the person you were yesterday," and "if there is nothing wrong with you then there is something wrong with you." Those two sentences hit home to me, and what I took away from Eddie Johnson's speech was to always remember and love who you are; but also know that you have the opportunity to always better yourself and learn if you so choose to, no matter your background!

Back to the three common misconceptions about bullying, often perpetuated by the media. The fact of the matter is that bullying is not always portrayed properly in the media, just like so many other topics. Often so-called "reality" television shows fuel our views of the world, when in actual reality, the producers have much more control over what happens than we realize. In fact, "reality TV" is hardly reality at all. It's drama that will get better ratings and therefore make more money! We don't often think about what the real truth might be, because the media has become a staple for the life of many people across the world. In truth, we fall victim to naivety by assuming that the media will properly portray events.

However, the media isn't entirely to blame. Many popular ideas are based upon stereotypes that have existed long before crazy reality shows. Those shows are just portrayals of our flawed reflections of our culture, which then work into our culture in terms of our expectations, and eventually work together to distort the truth. A popular saying that I constantly remind myself of is, "garbage in, garbage out." If you are constantly putting garbage into your thoughts you will probably end up putting garbage back out there—surround yourself with positive and good, and you will be much happier.

And what about the "official" definition of bullying, used by schools and in the workplace? The dictionary definition of bullying describes a person who repetitively harasses or intimidates smaller or weaker people. This textbook definition explains to us what one side of bullying can be, but it will not help us to become empathetic. It is also flawed because it states that the person being bullied is a smaller or weaker person. If your child is being bullied, it is not necessarily because she is smaller or weaker. In fact, if your child is being bullied, it is more important than ever that he does not believe that he is smaller or weaker, or this may exacerbate the emotional consequences.

My Story:

When I was a freshman in high school, I was about five foot four inches tall and weighed maybe 110 pounds soaking wet, so when kids called me small or tiny I realized quickly that if I showed that their comments bothered me, it would only happen more often and harder. The key to nipping that in the buttocks was that I had the confidence that I was just as good and in some ways bigger than the bigger kids picking on me.

Definitions like those used by many schools and textbooks may lead us down the wrong path and fog our understanding of what bullying is. To truly understand what it is, we must ask the kids who experience it. Here are a couple comments from kids in grammar school when asked about bullying in school:

"Bullying happens every day from 8 o'clock to 3 o'clock, people don't hit me, but they call me names and tease me. I don't feel good when they do it."

"I don't know why others pick on me, they think I am different because I have red hair and have glasses. I just want to be like them and not get called names."

Those experiencing it best define bullying. You may find it challenging to place a definition on an emotional experience if you have never had it before. Would you be able to explain love and feel that you have done a good job of it if you have never experienced it? This is precisely why the best way to define bullying is by talking with those who have gone through it. Only then can we make our best effort to understand what the child—or adult—is going through.

Try not to jump in and fix it, listening is much more useful at first. Not only will this help you to understand what she's going through but if the bullying victim is a child, then having the child help in the solution will have much better long term effects on him, and will reinforce him with confidence he'll need in the future, such as the confidence I had freshman year in high school. Teach your children that in most cases kids lash out on and bully the ones they fear or want to be like; jealousy is when you count the blessings of someone else and not yourself, and jealousy almost always turns into hate.

Is Your Child at Risk of Being Bullied?

Before we can fully understand how to solve bullying or understand the signs of your child being bullied, we must first figure out whether you should be suspicious. What I mean by being suspicious is, to know whether your child is more likely than others to be bullied at school and why. By understanding the risk, the proper level of action may be taken and you can prepare yourself to be alerted for the signs that your child may use to indicate that he is being bullied.

Keep in mind that just because your child is at risk of being bullied, it does not mean that she has a less likely chance of being successful. Success inevitably comes from within, with happiness. Happiness comes from many different places for many different people, but it often comes from love. This could be through having enough financial security to live comfortably and the freedom to do as you please, or more importantly and effectively, by having a supportive, loving family, which is what I have always been blessed to have and try to promote with everyone I meet. Every child has the potential to be happy, regardless of how others perceive him or her. Therefore, even the bullied child has just as much potential as any other to achieve success. The key is to constantly show and give children your unconditional love.

My Story:

When I was in school I had an English teacher who constantly put me down, telling me that I would end up working a low wage dead end job because I didn't put the effort in. Listening to her say that to me should have bothered me but since I had such a great family and friends that showed me how to love and have confidence in myself, I was able to let those nasty words from the teacher roll right off my back and into the gutter where they belonged, not me!

Now let's consider what aspects make children more likely to be bullied. To do this, let's try some thinking exercises with some rather abstract examples. I have deliberately chosen situations that are not from the school playground, as considering something in an entirely different context can be a useful tool that avoids any presuppositions. Remember, I am trying to rebuild your concept of bullying.

First, let us look at the zebra. They are often found in packs and typically have striped skin. Having striped skin does not make the zebra any better than one that happens to not have stripes because we have not defined what a "correct" zebra is. We just assume that zebras should look like the pictures we see in the nature books of them and how they look on television.

Regardless of your beliefs held, one thing is certain. You will notice the zebra without stripes in the herd! Predators may notice this zebra too and attack it because it stands out from the rest of the zebras. It is not the norm, but being the norm is not always right. And note, it is not necessarily the weaker animal that is attacked, but the one that is not conforming to the norm.

Another incident that from the animal kingdom involves coyotes. A coyote often hunts to lure animals into its trap so that it may attack it in isolation. The coyote may be resistant if the other animal is in a group surrounded by other animals of the same species that may defend it. An animal that is traveling in isolation from the group is at higher risk of being lured into the coyote's trap and is attacked when least expected, and this is the same with kids and people—this is why it is always smart to stay in groups, especially in unknown or busy places. The animal or person in isolation is not weaker or inferior compared to others in the pack, but is simply in isolation.

Think of the coyote as the bully and the bullied child as one who is isolated from the group. You may similarly think of the zebra as any given school child. Is your child the one in isolation? Are they the zebra without stripes? The answer cannot always easily be answered, unless your child looks physically different from the other children. If your child is more obese than the other children, substantially shorter, or even just has an unusual hair color, they can be susceptible to differentiation. But remember that just because your child is different than the norm, it doesn't mean that they are inferior by any means.

My Story:

A great example of this was the cutest girl in my 5th grade class. She was overweight and picked on by the popular girls, and some of the other kids who were trying to fit in with them. They would call her "Big Foot" and slam their feet down when the teacher wasn't looking.

This girl was bullied to no end. I and others would try to stop it and would tell her to ignore those kids, but it still affected her. I saw her 20 years later and spoke to her about it. She told me that it bothered her so much and was so engrained into her thoughts that she ended up going into the medical field to help others who felt weak or sick.

Any attribute that your child may have that alters his behavior or physical appearance may make him susceptible to the white zebra effect. If this is the case, you should investigate the situation further. Are people treating your child differently when you are around him or her? If people are treating your child differently in public, they may also be treated differently within the school or on the playground.

Even if your child is not perceived as having a physical or behavioral difference, he or she is still susceptible to bullying. A child who has few friends compared to his average classmates, or who does not identify with a specific group in school or cliques can be much more vulnerable. A good way to find out is to simply ask how many friends that she has or how many friends do most of the students have. If your child is more of a loner, like I was and to some extent, still am, then she may be more vulnerable to the types of bullying we are discussing.

A standard "I don't know" may be a typical answer but if that happens you could approach the situation from a different angle. If your child is in high school, ask her what groups there are and which one she belongs to. Generally, larger high schools have more groups and it is easier for a child to identify with one. Another indication may be if friends never ask to visit your home and your child never asks to attend social gatherings. The more involved we are with friends and groups, the more likely we will feel connected and less alone.

> ***The key is to constantly show and give children your unconditional love.***

The Evils of Cyber Bullying

It has only been a little over ten years since we first started noticing a dramatic growth in internet communication. The internet as a remote communication and collaboration tool was used by the United States government long before it became publicly available, but it is used today for nearly every purpose imaginable. One of these purposes is to communicate with people, often with personal information, saving us the time that it would normally take to call them or meet in person. Just about everyone has the internet and even carries it with them on their phones.

The internet is an amazing tool but it is also a very dangerous place. It is very easy to tarnish someone's reputation over the internet, or to post very powerful emotionally damaging comments to or about someone. If you haven't grown up in the online age, you may find it challenging to imagine how reading a particular piece of text, or being shunned online can be equally as hurtful to someone who is experiencing it as a face-to-face encounter. The danger of the matter is if we perceive these issues to be secondary to real-time bullying.

Cyber bullying falls victim to this way of thinking and is even more dangerous because it is the silent ghost, often outside of adult supervision and cameras. It is bullying that takes place on popular social networking sites such as Facebook, Instagram, Twitter, blogs and so on. During my research in writing this book I was amazed at how much bullying goes on right under our noses, in our own homes, because of the unlimited access of the internet we give to our children. I know that there is a fine line between privacy and trust, but it is also important to keep an eye on what your kids are doing online; remember the saying "garbage in, garbage out."

Negative comments or gossips can disrepute children in front of the peers who they must then go on to face in reality the next day at school. "Conventional" bullying and cyber bullying can therefore work together to send a student hurtling down into a vicious cycle that can be difficult (but possible) to break. It should not be taken lightly and should be prevented at all costs through your regulation. I have spoken to far too many people who have become depressed by what they have had to deal with due to online bullying.

Remember that you are in control of your children's privacy, although no doubt much to their annoyance as they grow older. You must help them to understand that it is for their own good, and that you will not allow them to navigate the internet completely alone, just as you wouldn't send them across town at two a.m. by themselves to go get you a snack at the store. Even if your children have nothing to hide or conceal from you, they may still not support you looking at their personal emails and social media accounts. The truth is, you should not have to. The key is to establish honesty and a relationship built on trust. You must always first show someone that you can trust her before you ask her to trust you. It is this unspoken mutual relationship that should be developed with your child, alongside conversation on how to handle cyber bullying events.

Michelle's Story:

When my children were old enough to go online, at first they were only permitted to do so on a family computer located in the living room of our home. When they were older and had computers in their bedrooms, my husband and I had them sign a contract with us. In the contract it stated key safety points we'd all agreed upon, such as, never to put their real address online, and that my husband and I were always to be given passwords. Not that we've had to use them to "spy" on our kids, but we needed to have them in case a situation arose.

Cyber bullying can be a challenging concept for many parents to grasp because it is relatively recent and they have not had to experience it in the past. I know I didn't have to deal with it growing up. My biggest fear was having to hop the fence in grammar school and getting into a fight at the empty Jehovah's Witness Hall after school. You may have known bullies or even have been bullied as a child, but not have experienced cyber bullying and therefore might have a challenging time grasping it as a concept—I know I didn't quite grasp it until I'd researched it quite a bit.

What are the differences between cyber bullying and offline bullying? Is cyber bullying as bad as offline bullying, or worse? How are cyber bullying and offline bullying similar? Let's consider each of these questions to give you a full understanding of what the difference between cyber bullying and offline bullying is:

Cyber bullying takes place online, whereas offline bullying takes place in person, and often at school and/or public gatherings. Cyber bullying can occur wherever children gather online, which can include online games that they play with strangers and peers, Facebook or other social networking sites, emails, and any new social gathering sites that did not exist while this book was being written. The malls, the record stores, parks, burger joints, and other hangouts of the 1950's to the 1990's are being replaced by online social gatherings. Very simply, the world is becoming "digitized."

One of the main differences is that offline bullying can be physical, while cyber bullying is not yet physically harmful. However, they can work off one another and spark physical harm if the child does not handle the cyber bullying properly.

Cyber bullying is similar to offline bullying in that they are both damaging and degrading. Words can be painful and students can be emotionally hurt because of them. Their names can also become blackened overnight. It is also subject to the same laws as the white zebra effect and the coyote hunting effect. Students who have fewer friends on a social media website may be more susceptible to being bullied, just as they would be offline. Similarly, children who are perceived as being different—such as having unusual interests, being gay or transgender (LGBT+), coming from an uncommon environment, or being against the "norm" in other ways are more likely to be bullied.

Offline bullying and cyber bullying are also similar in that the same bully may torment the child during school hours and through technology. A bully may verbally and physically harm a child during school hours, and then continue to do so online when the child is seemingly safe at home.

Another big and worrisome problem is that online bullying can sometimes come from complete strangers. Online gaming programs such as Xbox Live enable children to play their game systems with anyone around the world and to communicate with them as if they were on the telephone. This is a staggering breakthrough and is enjoyed by millions. The downside is that this opens up access for online bullies, often called "trolls," people who actively seek out others to torment online. Trolling is different than some other forms of online bullying because there is often no selection process. Instead, the users are often selected at random through usernames or screen names. As ridiculous as it may sound, it occurs online every day and is prevalent on social media and gaming websites. However, this is not as powerful as bullying on social networking websites by local peers, since the unknown bully does not know the user and therefore their attacks are not as personal.

To protect against trolling, the safest thing to do is not to share personal information. Anytime personal information is divulged may be portrayed as difference and the troll can take that information to formulate an emotionally hurtful statement. The statement becomes more hurtful if the information is personal, but is less harmful if it is more generalized and can be applied to others. This is because it is not so much the statement itself that hurts but the feeling of social rejection from peers that leaves the receiver feeling badly.

As we have discussed so far, there are many common similarities between online and offline bullying. Therefore, you can take heart knowing that the applications given in this book to preventing bullying are largely universal and can be applied to many different situations. As we move into the next chapter, please continue to think long-term. For instance, a "quick fix" of getting fast Facebook friends to give a fake impression of popularity or pushing the child into hobbies they have no interest in are no ways to solve this challenge. We must think very carefully about it and not rush to take action when a larger time commitment may be more successful for the long run.

While cyber bullying can be an extension of bullying that happens offline, a continuation of what goes on in school, or on the playground; it can also be separate, and even something that comes from complete strangers. Bullying that happens in real life crosses over quickly to the internet, where bullies can create legions of fake identities, befriend their victims, and use their discussions and confidences against them later.

There have even been cases of adults bullying children online, creating profiles as if they are contemporaries, and spreading lies and gossip about the victim because of some childish vendetta on the adult's part.

Megan's Story:

One such incident was in the news after young Megan, of St. Charles, MO, hung herself in her bedroom closet only weeks before her 14th birthday as the result of a barrage of horrifying MySpace messages. It all began when the mother of one of Megan's former friends took the time to create a profile of a teen boy and befriended Megan. After Megan developed an enormous crush on him, the fake boy the woman had created turned on her for "not being nice to her friends." The insults poured in and escalated, calling her a slut, saying everyone knew who she was and hated her. Her mother was aware of the situation and told her daughter repeatedly to shut the computer off, but like most teens, Megan found it impossible to walk away.

Not often knowing who is really behind things that are said online makes the bullies more vicious than they might be in person. It also gives a forum to those who might not have the courage to bully face to face. It allows predators to act like bullies, but remain cowards. Cyber bullying can reach a child any time of the day or night. It can happen when the child is alone and most vulnerable, and with smartphones so prevalent there is no time or place where children are not followed by the victimization.

Damaging posts about an adolescent can be hurtful words, gossip, or photos that are real or doctored via Photoshop, or another altering program or video. They can be private but more often are spread to ruin the life of the victim. These hateful and hurtful posts are difficult, if not impossible to remove. Not only does this continue to follow the victim any time someone searches their name, but having the proof of their being bullied as something tangible makes it even easier to obsess on, checking again and again for new views or comments.

While the internet may increase the likelihood of bullying and victimization, it can also be a shelter from the storm. Children who are bullied in real life are likely to use the internet to connect to new groups of people who do not know them offline. Here they can attempt to escape the shadow of bullying by finding groups and friends in any number of ways. They may seek out sites specifically designed to fight bullying or suicide prevention sites. They could join fan sites for their favorite shows, celebrities, or sports teams; or become members of communities of people interested in any number of hobbies or careers. In some cases this can be a very healthy way to gain confidence and convince the adolescent that there is nothing wrong with her, and that there are others with whom she shares much in common. However, all too often, the child may begin to interact online with someone who does not have his best interests in mind.

Like anything else, there are positives and negatives to being online, and it is up to parents and guardians to watch for the signs a child gives off. While some adults shut down when their teens talk about their celebrity crushes or online spats between friends, it is better to listen closely and encourage your child to discuss his online activities. Children who are being bullied online will spend as much time on their computer as those who are enjoying new friendships, perhaps even more. Do not expect them to avoid the computer if they are being cyber bullied. Instead they may be more agitated, depressed, combative, or secretive after time online.

One unexpected type of cyber bullying is self-bullying. Teens create a profile aside from their own and use it to send abusive messages to themselves. In some cases it is a way of putting their own horrible feelings about themselves out there, validating them for themselves. They feel worthless, ugly, or stupid; and like teens who self-harm they use words instead of blades to cut themselves down. Some do it in hopes that others will defend them. They look for support from others who will dispute the terrible things they feel to be true. When this works it can lead to an addiction to playing the victim.

After a time, no one will come to their defense because though it may not come to light that they started the bullying themselves, their constant attention-seeking via their victim status will become exhausting and exasperating to those who truly wish to help. They begin to believe that their own negative messages are true and become angry with anyone who suggests they walk away from, rather than feed into the cycle. In some cases those who begin the bullying are further depressed to find no one comes to their aid, instead finding messages that underscore the hurtful words they posted themselves. There is a case in the United Kingdom of a girl who bullied herself online for more than a year, posting that she should drink bleach, go kill herself, etc.,. Only after she committed suicide did investigators come to believe that the messages of hate had come from the teen herself.

Despite the disastrous repercussions, most kids see cyber bullying as a fact of life. Half of all teens and adolescents have either been bullied or have bullied someone else online. One third have had threats made against them on the internet. Depending on the study cited, the percentage of children who report bullying to a parent or another adult changes, but all studies I have read show it to be much fewer than 50%. Even fewer incidents are reported to the law. Until cyber bullying is seen widely as a critical situation facing our children, it will only continue to grow.

Cyber bullying is similar to offline bullying in that they are both damaging and degrading.

Words can be painful and students can be emotionally hurt because of them. Their names can also become blackened overnight.

Recognizing If Your Child is Being Bullied

Parents and caretakers are frequently unaware that children are being bullied. Children will rarely bring up the bullying on their own and many times will even deny it is happening. There are a number of reasons why children will hide their victim status. But although children do not always verbally tell their parents that they are suffering from bullying, there are several non-verbal cues you can watch for. When you understand the signs you can be more aware, thus honing in on your "bully radar" in the home and at the school.

If you or someone that you know was bullied in school, you may already recognize the signs that your child is being bullied. Maybe you just don't know it yet. Either way, here are some of the indicators you should look out for:

Unexplainable Injuries:

Injuries will most likely be visible on the arms or face. If you believe that your child has injuries, you may want to casually ask her how they happened, and monitor the response for lies or discomfort. If Jack comes home with black and blue marks on his arm and says he fell up the stairs trying to get to class on time, ask for details. If he gets defensive he is probably trying to hide the fact that he is being tormented.

Lost or Destroyed Belongings:

Possessions that are claimed to be lost or "accidentally broken" may actually be evidence of the bullying. However, the child may devise excuses in order to avoid revealing the true situation. If Meg constantly needs new binders and school supplies, then she may be dealing with a bully who is taking her stuff.

Frequent "Headaches" or "Stomachaches" (Faking Illness):

A bullied child may claim to have pains or act as though they do so that his parents will allow him to miss school. Making a child go to school with reports of pains is subjective to the parent, but if these "symptoms" persist you probably want to investigate further. Let Eddie know that you are concerned and that you are setting up an appointment to see the doctor, it is not healthy to be getting sick so frequently. Talk to the doctor's office and let them know your concern about possible bullying, maybe the doctor can help Eddie by talking with him in private.

Changes in Eating Habits:

A child's eating habits may change because of the stress of bullying, but also because of skipping the school lunch from having her money or food stolen.

Additionally, if your child has limited friends he may be alone at lunch time and too embarrassed to eat his lunch, in fear he will be teased for sitting by himself. If your child appears to be abnormally hungry after school, you might want to ask questions such as what she had for lunch, or ask the school to monitor your child's food purchases.

My Story:

I remember a time when my friend, Mary, was being bullied at lunch. Another girl, Megan, was taking Mary's sandwiches and throwing them in the trash while laughing. The lunchroom staff was too busy to notice but finally I got so fed up seeing my classmate be harassed, that I took Megan's books and lunch and threw them in the trash. I just couldn't understand how someone could laugh while hurting anyone—it made no sense to me then or now. Years later I see that I went about helping the wrong way but as a child we don't always see the big picture. It is adults' job to help kids to learn common sense approaches to difficult situations and people. We need to show kids through example and lessons.

Stress often causes a lack of eating in the short-term and overeating in the long-term. If the child appears not to be hungry for meals, it may indicate stress that could be the result of bullying. Additionally, if you make him a packed lunch before school, check his lunchbox when he returns home. If it is still full, then you may have a bullying situation going on.

Difficulty Sleeping:

Nightmares and unusual sleep disruptions may occur if kids have experienced unpleasant situations during the day. Sleep habits should be compared against periods when bullying was not suspected, as some kids are just naturally more likely to have nightmares or trouble sleeping.

My Story:

When I was eleven or so I watched a really scary movie, The Shining, and couldn't sleep for about a week, and needed to leave the light on for the entire night. In a sense that movie was the bully that scared me, but looking back on that experience I know the importance of sleep and how our minds will keep us awake when there is stress, nervousness, or just plain fear! Fear will affect our sleep patterns more than anything else.

Declining Academic Performance:

Because bullying can be stressful, especially at school, it can occupy the child's mind instead of school work. It may cause her to dislike or even spite school, not because of the workload, but because of the atmosphere.

Scott's Story:

Scott was always a top notch, A+ student whom the teachers loved and adored, he would always raise his hand when the teacher asked questions. Suddenly in the 5th grade, Scott started to have declining grades and would sit further back in the classroom. The teachers were concerned and kept an eye on him, they would ask him if he was okay but he shrugged it off. During gym class the teacher noticed he wouldn't change into his gym shorts or participate most days, so the teacher reached into Scott's bag to force him into playing and found his clothes were soaked. Upon further investigation, the teacher found a group of classmates were throwing Scott's clothes into the toilet. When the kids were confronted by the authorities and asked why they were tormenting Scott they simply responded "that it was fun" and "they were bored."

Bullying isn't easily understood but through research and reading up on the subject hopefully we can teach others how destructive it is to everyone involved. I've researched this subject for years and have spoken to countless numbers of people who have been bullied, are being bullied, or are the bullies themselves; and I am still amazed at how many times I hear those two responses.

Loss of Friends and Avoiding Social Situations:

Bullying can be detrimental to self-confidence and lead to social isolation at school. The lack of self-confidence can be seen in social situations, possibly leading to a loss of friends, making the child socially inept. This scenario is one that often occurs as a result of bullying over the long-term, but with help from you, he can learn to prevent and beat bullying and avoid these long-term consequences. In Scott's situation the gym teacher was alert, and was able to stop the bullying fairly quickly by finding the wet gym clothes and being proactive in the resolution of the situation, unfortunately this isn't always the case. Let's say Scott's teacher didn't find the wet clothes and the kids kept bullying Scott. It would be likely that the bullying would continue and get worse. Other kids and even friends would find out, some would want to be "included" with the bully crowd to fit in and feel protected from the bullies by joining in, or it could go the other way—Scott might have felt defeated and started bullying others. "If you can't beat them then join them" comes to mind and the bullying problem would then grow. Even though Scott was a great kid, and was considered a "love bug" or "happy go lucky kid," he didn't see any other option, just like when I threw Megan's stuff into the trash! I will touch on that scenario in another chapter.

Feelings of Helplessness:

Indications of helplessness may arise if the kid becomes less optimistic towards finding solutions to problems. Some examples include giving up easier on math problems or getting easily frustrated when facing mundane tasks. If you notice that Troy is getting frustrated with helping with simple chores such as emptying the dishwasher or straightening up the home when he has always loved helping in the past, or if he is starting to slip on doing his homework, then there is probably something going on in school or in his life that he isn't talking about. As adults we sometimes forget that kids and teenagers have a much more difficult time expressing their emotions, unless they are angry emotions (they usually blurt out those)! They are still learning a lot about life and we sometimes forget that. Kids are sponges and they often react in the same manner that they see in their environment, which is why we must keep our emotions in check and teach by example—they see us as the leaders we should be. We often forget that, especially in the early years of life, their family is their world. One of my favorite clichés is "don't try to change the world but change our world." Changing our outlook on life is contagious, just like laughter!

Self-Destructive Behavior:

Behavior that is considered to be self-destructive would include mental or emotional harm to oneself. This could be running away from home, talking about suicide, inflicting physical harm, or talking poorly about oneself. All self-destructive behavior should be taken seriously; the cause sought out with diligence and solved with action.

Adam's Story:

"Adam" is a teenager who'd attempted suicide twice. He told me that he left all kinds of hints for his family. He would text his friends with pictures of himself pointing a fake gun to his head, he would post on social media how he wished he were dead, and would cut himself where it could be seen by everyone… but when he felt no one was taking the time to ask him about these "clues," he felt

that bad attention was better than no attention at all and took a bottle of sleeping pills. He told me that later on he felt guilty and wished he didn't put his family through that ordeal, but that he felt better knowing that "they really did care but just didn't know how to express it." He asked me to be sure that I told every parent reading my book "to know that most kids just want the approval of their parents and when they are too busy to notice what is going on, then the kid is probably going to act too busy for them." What great advice!

Remember that all of this behavior can be the result of a multitude of factors, having nothing at all to do with bullying. Many of them can be a result of personality factors, stress caused by other events or even just growing older. Noticing several elements together may cause more reason to be suspicious that your child is being bullied. While the concerned parent or loved one should not assume that these signs are definitely the result of bullying, we must pay attention if we're to conquer the bullying challenge.

Uncovering Additional Information:

If you are attempting to uncover whether or not your kid is being bullied, he or she does not need to be the only source of information. In fact, it is best to investigate the problem by observing it from many different angles in order to gain a detailed insight into the evidence. Classmates and school staff are great sources if approached carefully and in a non-threatening manner.

Remember that kids don't want to be considered "narks" or "snitches," and school authorities are often afraid of lawsuits—in this day and age, because there are so many silly lawsuits out there over nonsense, they are careful how they react to both students and parents. When I was a kid my principal used to tell me to step into his office if I was in trouble. I knew that if he said to close his door and then lit a cigarette, I was about to get after-school detention or mop cleaning of the library.

The student's friends and classmates can often be an excellent resource. Your kid may sometimes be afraid, or feel ashamed to tell you that he is being bullied; but his friends may already know. If you believe that your child would be upset at you for investigating her personal life, you can ask indirect questions. For example, instead of asking if your child is being bullied, ask his classmate if there is a bully at the school. If the answer is "yes," continue by asking who he or she bullies, and what he or she does. The student may not name your child, but you may be able to match descriptions of what the bully does with signs that your child has exhibited. If your kid's possessions are broken constantly and the bully has a reputation for breaking stuff, then that might not be a coincidence.

Some schools take a more proactive approach to bullying, whereas others, sadly, just ignore it completely. Unfortunately, schools are polarized, and it doesn't matter the location or level of education. Differences abound, from the elementary schools in America to high schools in England. If your child's school is willing to work with you, you may ask them if your child has ever mentioned anything that may indicate that he is being bullied. Similar questions may also be asked to classmates or you could ask the school to silently monitor the bullying environment. Most people who choose to work with kids as teachers and administrators do so because they love kids. Sometimes what happens is that they are so overwhelmed and overworked that they become numb to the issues, or simply don't have the time. Here is an unrelated example but I think it will help with what I am saying:

My Story:

I was a volunteer with Hospice for a long time and I did a lot of "death bed vigils" but after many years at this difficult job, it became routine. I felt I was losing my empathy toward the patient and death didn't seem to faze me any longer. I was too close to it to realize that I was becoming numb to death until it happened to someone I dearly loved. Sometimes we need to remind people in every type of job—whether it be teaching, nursing, cooking, or even policing—why they chose the career path they took and that reminder is all it takes for them to resume caring, appropriately. I like to say that "sometimes I missed something because I was too far into the woods" in a situation—sometimes we need to step out of the woods in order to see the true picture.

Finding information can be challenging but it is well worth it. Never assume anything. It is also important to approach the information rationally before taking actions. Remember that even if your child is being bullied, if the facts are not available, you may begin to discredit yourself if you continuously go to the school without hard evidence to present. A solid fact includes firsthand information like a testimonial from your child or a classmate, for instance. It may even be one of your own observations, or an audio or visual recording. No matter what evidence you may have, the key is that the information comes directly from the source. Information gathered loosely from a friend, but denied by your child, will not fare well as it is considered hearsay. Tangible information will always be the most powerful

A bully will make the child feel it is his own fault he has been targeted. She may believe there is something fundamentally wrong with her, and begin to believe the bullying is something she brought on herself and deserve. In other instances, the child may believe the involvement of adults will only reinforce his personal weakness and he will strive to find a solution on his own in an attempt to regain his personal power. I know that I would have dreaded seeing my Mom at my school trying to find out why Dave and I were getting into fights, I would have worried that the other kids would make fun of me calling me a "mama's boy," but times have changed and parent involvement in schools and with their kids' activities have been much more welcome. A visit to the school by my Mom nowadays would probably go unnoticed by my peers and wouldn't be as big of a deal.

A kid who is already isolated and feeling alone may feel that no one will understand, or that if she exposed the bullying to others it might draw attention to her flaws. The kid may fear the adult will tell him that he is being weak and side against him, or even punish him for not being able to "take a joke," or stand up for himself. Bullying is not harmless fun, nor is it a way to teach kids to "toughen up" or to stand up for themselves. It can be deadly: Suicide is the third leading cause of death according to the Center for Disease Control. It results in about 4,400 deaths per year. According to a study by Yale University, bullied victims are seven to nine percent more likely to consider suicide.

It is the responsibility of all adults who have a relationship with a child, whether they are family, a caretaker, a physician or any other authority figure, to recognize the signs that the child is being bullied, and then to take the correct actions to support the child. The internet is full of excellent advice and stories to help you determine whether you should be concerned about your kid being bullied (see "Resources" at the end of this book to get you started). I have spent countless hours on the internet and read books of all sorts during my research for this book, along with interviewing everyday people like yourself in order that you and I could learn from each other and all of us help to overcome bullying. We can all work together to be part of the solution!

What follows is a partial list of the most common things to watch for, including summarizations of some of the things we've examined already:

• A kid who is being bullied may begin to have more frequent injuries, bumps, bruises, etc.; she may struggle to explain the injuries or try to hide them, or have preposterous stories as to how they occurred. This on its own is not concrete evidence; when children are growing they sometimes become clumsy as their bodies change and aren't really sure how or why they are tripping over their own feet.

• If a kid is losing or breaking his belongings often, and again, trying to hide this or not able to explain how these things have happened. It may be that a bully is taking or breaking his things. Take note whether the kid is careless with her belongings at home or whether the loss or damage of items occurs only when she is at school, the playground, or another specific place.

• Bullying can happen on the bus ride to and from school by older kids that the child does not normally see during the rest of the day. In this case, the child may intentionally miss the bus, or beg for rides to and from school.

• If your kid is complaining of headaches or stomachaches, or appears to be pretending to be ill when he is scheduled to be in a particular place, this could be a sign of bullying. We will further discuss the physical repercussions of bullying in another chapter, but it is important to note that the child may actually be feeling sick from the constant fear of the tormentor and is not necessarily faking to get out of the situation.

• Kids may have a dramatic change in their eating habits. Some may binge eat in an attempt to self-console, while others may not have an appetite at all. Something else to watch for is if a child comes home from school very hungry. She may have had her lunch taken or could have avoided the lunchroom all together in order to hide from peers. I still remember the feeling of walking into the lunch room my first year in high school. I was scared out of my mind because I didn't know anyone in there and feared having to sit alone or be rejected. It is a scary place if you are shy or awkward, and in most cases a kid would never admit to the fear, especially if he or she is being bullied already.

• Kids who have always slept through the night easily may have a difficult time falling asleep or may begin to experience nightmares on a regular basis or begin wetting the bed.

• A noticeable decline in the ability to concentrate as well as declining grades may indicate that a kid is being bullied.

• Look for statements like "there was drama" or "kids were messing around with me" when your child talks about his or her day. These can be code words for bullying.

• Children who no longer come home with stories about their friends or who avoid social situations when they used to dive right in may be reacting to the isolation of bullying.

• Older kids and teens showing signs of agitation or melancholy after spending time online may be the victims of cyber bullies.

• If your child is coming home at a time normally scheduled for extracurricular activities such as sports or clubs, and saying they're cancelled for the day or have been cut altogether, you may want to call the school to check whether this is true or if your kid has elected to refrain from attending.

• Children who are victims of bullying will often begin to exhibit signs of lower self-esteem. A child who has always been self-confident may begin to say "I can't" when asked to try new things, or decline when asked to offer opinions. He will close himself off from any opportunity for failure because he is being conditioned to believe he cannot succeed. She may also take the blame for anything that goes wrong, thinking she cannot do anything right.

• Some kids may become sullen or sad with no apparent reason, and the mood does not go away. Others may become angry or even aggressive, and may begin to lash out at younger siblings in an effort to exercise some control.

• Your child may wait to use the bathroom until he gets home in order to avoid being cornered in the restrooms at school, which are by and large poorly monitored.

• It is not unheard of to see some regression, such as asking for help with tasks they previously completed on their own. Additionally, you may find your child becomes more dependent, or "clingier," and has anxiety when she is separated from you. He may need constant reassurance that you want to be close to him and will never leave him, and if they make a mistake, he may react as though he does not expect to be loved or forgiven.

• Older children and teens who have their own phones may become upset after checking their messages, but not want to talk about why they're upset.

• Kids may seek to further isolate themselves by running away, or attempting to run away, believing they are not worthy of being part of the family or group, or in an effort to remove themselves from the bullying situation.

• Some kids may begin to hurt themselves and may even attempt suicide.

Joe's Story:

One of my most challenging email interviews was with a kid from a rural farm town in the Midwest who I'll call, "Joe." Joe responded to a post on Facebook and felt compelled to tell his story about being bullied because of his lazy eye. The bullying got so bad that he started to "cut himself" on his arms just to feel the distraction of external pain instead of the agony of his internal pain. In order to forget about the bullies at school, he dropped out of baseball and started working with his Dad on the farm. The bullying eventually stopped, but the lesson Joe wanted to pass along was "it may never feel like it will end, hurting yourself only makes it worse and once you realize you are stronger and they are only the tough guy wimps leaching on others pains, you will beat them by not hurting yourself or them but, by becoming stronger." Joe's advice is perfect!

This has by no means been an exhaustive list. You know your kids best. Any change in behavior or routine that seems worrying to you should be treated seriously and immediately.

Bullying is not harmless fun, nor is it a way to teach kids to "toughen up" or to stand up for themselves. It can be deadly:

Suicide is the third leading cause of death according to the Center for Disease Control. It results in about 4,400 deaths per year.

The Short-Term Impacts of Bullying

The impacts of bullying are wide spread and long lasting. Let's begin with the immediate effects of a bully's actions. Many of these will crossover with the signs that you or your child is being bullied. Some people hide these things better than others, so even if you do not see them, it may still be happening.

For children and teens their education is affected to a large degree. According to dosomething.org, an average of 160,000 teens skip school each day because of bullying. When these victims do go to school, they have difficulty paying attention and their grades suffer because of it. It can be nearly impossible to focus on new information when you are in fear of your peers and what they will do next. Adults who are victims of workplace bullying will use most of their sick time to remove themselves from a situation, finding it difficult to concentrate on their tasks when at work.

Depression and anxiety are the most common result of bullying in any form. The inability to stop the bullying, and the secret worry that you lack something others have and everyone else knows, causes many people to become depressed. Endless, looping rumination on specific occurrences reinforces the anxiety felt when the bullying occurs. It can be difficult for people who have not experienced bullying to understand the constant fear in the mind of the victim, even when there is no sign of the bully around. It takes over your every thought and makes it impossible to relax, and enjoy time with friends and family.

A person's self-esteem takes a big hit when he is bullied. There is an overwhelming feeling of worthlessness that deepens when she is not able to make the bully stop, and she may even feel too ashamed to ask for advice or help, especially because it has been pounded into our heads as kids to "toughen up" or "don't be a wimp."

Tori's Story:

Tori was in the seventh grade and was being chased home every day by a group of older kids. He said he would cover up his black and blues with long sleeve shirts, and cry himself to sleep at night because he was so scared that his brothers would tease him even more, that he was "weak" or a "nerd." Looking back now, he admits that he was totally wrong about his brothers "not backing him up" and he regrets having stayed silent.

A lesson I have learned in life is that we forget that kids think totally different than us when it comes to problems. We must remind ourselves that they are lacking the years of experience we have with coping with problems, they are just learning. Sometimes we treat kids and teens as if they are seasoned adults, and expect them to "deal with" problems that they simply don't have the experience to cope with.

Some victims may try to change their look and/or personalities in order to either appease the bully, or to blend in better with other students and avoid the confrontation altogether. If a child is being bullied because she is a good student, or a "teacher's pet" especially, she may try to get lower grades and act inappropriately in class to lose that stigma.

My Story:

I actually tried doing the tactic of trying to get lower grades and acting inappropriately in class when I was in the fifth grade, but I was lucky enough to have a really observant and caring principal, Mr. Charles Hayden. Mr. Hayden took me into his office and talked with me for a couple hours, just giving me life lessons, and was able to get what was bothering me out of me. Then, instead of going back to the bully and punishing him, he gave me advice how to stop it. The advice he gave me is woven into this book, along with advice and stories from everyday people just like you and I.

Even if they are bullied for other reasons, victims of bullying during the teen years tend to lose interest in academic achievements and are more prone to begin acting out in an inappropriate manner while in school or at home, sometimes dropping out of school completely.

Eating disorders are sometimes resultant of bullying and while this is more commonly reported in females, it is not unheard of in males as well. I have read many stories of boys trying to lose weight by vomiting or not eating at all.

Dave's Story:

When my personal trainer, "Dave," was a kid, he didn't know of any other way to slim down except by forcing himself to vomit after dinner. His Mom made unhealthy dinners and he was overweight his entire childhood. It wasn't until he was in college, and learned how to cook and eat properly that he regained his balance, and stopped starving himself by vomiting. He was so affected by his upbringing that he chose to become a personal trainer in order to help others who are going through what he struggled with for nineteen years.

Eating disorders can include anorexia and bulimia, but also overeating. Girls who are bullied in a sexual manner may gain weight in order to avoid unwanted attention to their physical self.

The inability to fall asleep at night is common in those who are bullied, both children and adults. When they do fall asleep, they can have vivid and disturbing nightmares which may or may not include the actual bully. The lack of good rest only adds to their anxiety and lack of focus during waking hours. Some children may begin wetting the bed, adding to their shame and lack of self-worth. The flip side of this is being emotionally worn-out and exhausted, and they may fall asleep when they are in places they feel safe. During a time when I was being bullied and was having terrible anxiety, I went to a movie with a few friends. It was E.T. (showing my age) and I'd been looking forward to it for weeks. I fell asleep only minutes into the movie and didn't wake up until it was over. This was years ago and I have still not seen the movie, because thinking of it brings me back to the anxiety I felt that night. When your mind becomes engaged in something other than the fear and worry, it is difficult to stay awake or attentive, and tasks such as driving can become dangerous because as you concentrate on the road, your tensions release and the exhaustion takes over.

The need to stay home from school or work is not solely fear-based. There are real physical and mental issues that result from being the victim of a bully, and feeling like there is no way to fight back or stop the behavior. Stress is a major contributor to many stomach ailments; especially ulcers, irritable bowel syndrome, and even colitis. Stress also lowers the effectiveness of the immune system, making the victim subject to colds, flu, and other illnesses. Aches and pains with no identifiable physical cause, sometimes believed to be fibromyalgia in adults, or "growing pains," in children, can result from the stress of being bullied. High blood pressure and chest pains from stress can end up costing the victim many medical tests and nights in the hospital as well as have a financial impact.

Jack's Story:

Jack, who is a bank teller at a small town bank, recalls being removed from his job via ambulance with astronomical blood pressure after being completely stressed out by a bullying coworker. Jack told me that the only way he was able to get his blood pressure back to normal was to remove himself from the bully. It was tough but he knew the stress would end up killing him. In the end, he quit his job and let his former boss know what was going on. The bank offered him a position in another town and his blood pressure almost immediately went back to normal, and he felt so much better.

Hormonal problems can begin with bullying, including issues with menstruation and lower libido. Victims who are stressed can experience both physical and mental numbness; have tingling in their fingers, toes, and lips; and may lose the ability to experience positive emotions, as if someone has dampened the experience of living. Seizures, athlete's foot, and even extreme thirst are all physical effects of stress that can be due to bullying. Anxiety and stress can cause symptoms that mimic any number of serious medical conditions, and not knowing what is wrong with them can make the victims even more upset and exacerbate the situation.

When you are the victim of a bully, you become forgetful and indecisive, and extremely emotional, possibly crying at the drop of a hat. There can be a sense of guilt where you have done nothing wrong, and you can be hypersensitive, taking perfectly normal comments as critical. There might be jaw clenching or grinding of your teeth, which adds to the probability of headaches. Victims can be fearful at all times and even become hyper-vigilant, mimicking the signs of paranoia.

As you can see, bullying's short-term effects are not to be taken lightly. If you are a victim of bullying, you should let your physician know this when visiting for a seemingly unrelated issue as it might help in finding what is really happening to you physically and mentally. Stress can take over your life, and even when you think you are handling it well, it can manifest itself in unexpected ways—trust me, I know from my own experiences and from corresponding with hundreds of victims, stress really is the number one killer of really nice people every day.

> *It can be difficult for people who have not experienced bullying to understand the constant fear in the mind of the victim.*

The Long-Term Impacts of Bullying

In the last chapter, we looked at the short-term effects of bullying, but the effects can stay with a person for his entire life. Professionals are becoming convinced that children who have been bullied relentlessly have problems into their adult lives that are similar to those of children that are abused in the home, and even display the symptoms of post-traumatic stress disorder. When children experience bullying, the long term effects can be mitigated by stopping the bullying quickly and helping the child through the process of healing, like my principal did for me in grammar school. If left unchecked, the depression and anxiety of being bullied can lead to chronic depression, leaving the victim sad or melancholy for years, exhausted all of the time, and unable to think straight or impaired in her ability to make decisions. She will feel hopeless, worthless, and guilty most of the time.

Bullying that continues for a length of time can be considered traumatic and victims can experience post-traumatic stress disorder. They may continue to fixate on the bullying for years after it has occurred. This feeling of unworthiness can spin itself into social anxiety and difficulty with new people. The victim may have a hard time making friends and connecting with peers. This continued isolation can lead him to fill the emptiness in unhealthy ways.

Theresa's Story:

Theresa was from a small town in Maine. She was being bullied by her co-workers at a part time job after school. The constant harassment and teasing got so bad that she started smoking. She had no outlet to relax and had vivid nightmares for weeks. When she finally got up the courage to tell the store manager of her bad treatment from the others, the manager immediately fired her and called her a "liberal brat who better grow a back bone, everyone gets teased." Unfortunately, some people don't realize how much words can hurt us—sometimes words are more hurtful than physical pain. Always remember that words can never be taken back, be wise with your words.

Kids may decide to run away, hiding from the bullies and the shame of not being able to stop them. Living on the streets is a devastating step further from recovery, and there is a likelihood of becoming involved in prostitution, drug addiction and trafficking, gangs, and other criminal and dangerous lifestyles. Adults may not run away physically, but they will find ways of coping that can be just as unhealthy.

Self-medicating can occur in many forms. Some people will shop, using "retail therapy" to make themselves feel better while creating serious financial challenges for themselves and their families. Since they have a difficult time bonding with other people, they may try to buy acceptance and love spending money they cannot afford on even the newest of acquaintances.

Money problems are more prevalent in young adults who have experienced bullying than those who have not. Others seek refuge in food, overeating and indulging in comfort foods to fill the empty void from their social lives, or else exercising such extreme control over their eating that they become anorexic.

Alcohol and drugs are a way to numb fear and temporarily escape anxiety, but will become an addiction quite easily. I didn't need to do research on this one, as I personally dealt with alcohol addiction for a long time. Alcohol is a depressant and will only bring the user down further, and while drugs will feel good when the user is doing them, afterward will contribute to the user's feelings of being unable to control herself and of being ashamed of herself. Bullying victims turn to drinking and drugs not solely to make the demons in their heads quiet down, but also as a way to connect with others. When one is altered, the social inhibitions are lowered and a person otherwise isolated can feel as though he is communicating better with new people. There is a sense of easy acceptance with alcoholics and addicts that can feel like paradise to someone who has been isolated for such a large part of their lives.

Self-harm is another method victims use to ease frustration, attempt to communicate the pain of bullying, and in some cases punish themselves for being bullied. Recent studies show that children who are bullied grow five times more likely to self-harm later in their adolescence. Self-harm can also be a sign that the teen is having thoughts of suicide and no longer wants to live.

Girls are more likely than boys to cut themselves, burn themselves, or cause physical harm to themselves in some other way.

Not all suicidal teens and adults self-harm. There are other clues to let you know someone is considering suicide. Listen in conversation for phrases such a "things would be so much better if I weren't here," or "I can't handle my life anymore." They may become overly interested in death or macabre things. People who have suicide on the mind may give their things away and begin saying their goodbyes to people. Reckless behavior is another sign that someone may no longer value their lives.

My Story:

I had suicidal thoughts for months on end when I was thirteen. My Dad had just died, school wasn't fun, and I just wanted to sit in my room, and snack on doughnuts and WaWa brand iced tea. I would ride my bike to the ocean by St. Gabriel Church and think about how much better off my family and I would be if I were to just drown myself. Luckily I had such a strong bond with my family and friends that I didn't go through with killing myself, but what I learned looking back is that most people didn't even catch on to how depressed I was because I held it all inside. The lesson here is to never assume someone is okay and to always tell your loved ones how much you love them, even if it is "corny" or "uncool."

There is often no outward sign that someone is having suicidal thoughts. Bullying victims are much more likely to consider or commit suicide than those who were never bullied. Suicide is the third highest cause of teen death in the United States with roughly 4,400 suicides annually. For every adolescent who has committed suicide, there are a 100 who have attempted it. Fourteen percent of young people admit they have had thoughts of suicide and seven percent have made at least one actual attempt. More than half of these suicides and attempts are connected to the bullying experience.

For those who make it past the teen years, serious, long lasting health issues can result from bullying and the stress caused from it. Researchers are beginning to link diabetes, allergies, asthma, chronic fatigue syndrome, multiple sclerosis, and even some types of cancer to stress. Bullying victims are six times more likely to be diagnosed with a serious illness, a psychiatric disorder, or to be smokers than those who were never bullied.

As adults, victims of either childhood or adult bullying have a difficult time keeping jobs. This can be due to the inability to form relationships, low self-esteem, fear of success, and health problems. The likelihood of becoming agoraphobic later in life is increased by roughly four times that of the kids who never had any experience with bullying. Adult victims of bullying are not immune to suicidal thoughts or actions either, whether they were bullied as children and still carry the scars, or whether the bullying began after adolescence, the number of suicide attempts and those experiencing suicidal thoughts are higher among bullying victims than those who have never had been bullying victims. To reiterate the statistics I showed before, a study has shown that those who have been bullied are seven to nine percent more likely to try suicide than those who have not.

> ***Bullying victims are six times more likely to be diagnosed with a serious illness, a psychiatric disorder, or to be smokers than those who were never bullied.***

What If Your Child Is the Bully?

Some people are naturally drawn to leadership and power. Our society—and really most societies—values those who possess the power to control money, things, and people. When someone does not have the correct tools to gain that power in a healthy way, he may turn to bullying. This is not a hard and fast rule. Not everyone who craves power and does not have the means to attain it becomes a bully.

Children who come from homes where aggression is the norm may be more likely to adopt aggressive behavior in their own lives, but again, this does not hold true for all children. Some children raised in aggressive homes will become internal and fearful. A number of things have to come together for bullying to flourish. The environment has to be conducive to the behavior. If there is a not a standard of behavior that everyone is held to at a school, the workplace, or anywhere else people gather, bullying has an opportunity to take hold.

Society as a whole, gives more attention to those who act out than those who are pleasant and respectful. Sitcoms, news stories, celebrities; so much of the focus of the media is on negative behavior. Justin Bieber is accused of egging his neighbor's house and it is not possible to turn on the television without seeing that story over and over again. Other celebrities are working with charities, or just living quiet, simple lives; they make music or movies as well as the Justin Biebers or Lindsay

Lohans, but they do not attain the same level of media frenzy when they leave their homes. Unfortunately, just like sex, sometimes negative and destructive behavior "sells" and is glamorized, and even rewarded at times.

Children who are jealous of the popularity of others or lack social skills may see the attention given to those who act up and mimic it, using other kids as fodder for their mischief. If this gets the reaction they are seeking, it may grow into full-blown bullying.

Vinny's Story:

Vinny from Scranton told me that he bullied his teachers by placing thumb tacks on the teacher's seats and gluing the locks shut on the doors, for one reason alone: "It was the only way I could get any attention from my Dad and bad attention is better than none at all, even if it meant playing Nintendo 64 in my room every day after school!"

If children do not get a loving atmosphere at home where sharing feelings is encouraged, they are more likely to bully others. They do not have an outlet for their emotions, and become angry and lash out. Also likely to bully are children who come from homes where discipline is inconsistent. My general rule is "do hugs not hits." Intolerance to other people at home will instill a belief in the child that she is "better than." She may go to school thinking that anyone different from her is a lesser person who "deserves" to be bullied. So, sometimes parents must ask themselves the hard question: "Am I a bully?"

For some, that one toe dip into the pool of bullying is distasteful enough that they do not continue, but others latch onto that feeling of power and refuse to let go. One unifying theme for all of those who bully repeatedly is a lack of empathy. A bully does not understand or care what his actions do to the victim beyond getting his own way. She enjoys being the mastermind, the puppeteer, and does not consider the feelings of others. He can also be aggressive with adults and authority figures.

Bullies in the workforce are frequently those who feel they are not getting enough recognition for the work they do. They taunt others who do not live up to their expectations in order to make themselves seem superior. Another workplace bully is someone who has been placed in a position he is not trained or suitable for, we will get to this later in the book. This type of person will bully those under them to cover their own incompetence and weakness.

Bullies rarely make a conscious effort to bully. Instead, they are opportunists and generally feel they are justified in their actions.

A bully chooses his/her victims in a number of ways:

• Those who are good at what they do can become targets for jealous bullies. The bullies may be afraid that their own talents are being out-shined and make a move toward marginalizing those who are successful.

• Gifted students or talented workers who move up quickly and go the extra mile for assignments can become targets for those who are less willing or able to compete. Instead of working harder, the bully makes the victim's life miserable, until they do not want to try and the playing field is leveled.

• People who already suffer from depression, anxiety, or low self-esteem are magnets for bullies who feed on their weakness to create their own power.

• Loners or those with only a few friends are easy prey for bullies who do not want the conflict of becoming the target of a group, again like going after the zebra with no stripes.

• People who are gaining popularity and thereby threatening the status of the bully may become victims to keep the status quo and stop anyone else from attempting a rise in position.

• Anyone with a "different" physical feature such as being tall, short, fat, thin, wearing glasses, etc., can attract the attention of a bully.
• People who are different from the group by ethnicity, religion, race, sexuality, or physical disability are often jumped on by bullies.

Clearly, there are as many reasons for bullying as there are bullies and victims. By reviewing the topic we may be able to help with stopping the bullying in our lives or the lives of others, another one of my favorite sayings is "don't try to change the world, try to change our world." By changing our own surroundings and our small circles we will help to change more than we might ever imagine.

> *Society as a whole, gives more attention to those who act out than those who are pleasant and respectful.*

Reacting to Bullying

It can be one of the most difficult situations to get out of, but there are methods to try to make a bully stop her actions. How you react to a bully can greatly influence whether he continues. Not every technique will work with every bully, so it's good to have a number of options in your arsenal.

First, children (and adults) who are being bullied should try the following:

Remember that this is not your fault. Nothing you have said or done gives someone else the right to bully you. They will attempt to make you feel guilty, but you need to stay strong and not allow them to undermine your self-worth.

Even if your response is one of anger, the bully will be satisfied that she was able to get under your skin. A better reaction, particularly if the bully is someone you have just met, is to be very kind to him. This is not a sure thing, but sometimes bullies have been treated poorly in the past and do not expect kindness from strangers. Your bully may be intimidated by a new face and worried that you will replace her in the group. There is no reason to go overboard. You don't need to pander to him, just wish him a good morning or include him in a conversation. If after a few tries she is not changing her negative behavior, then stop. She may begin to assume through your kindness that her nasty ways are acceptable to you. Meet his negative comments head on. Look him directly in the face and don't hide from him. Use an assertive tone of voice but be careful not to be threatening. Call her behavior out into the light. Let her know you see what she is trying to do and you want her to stop—sometimes just saying "no" or "stop" is enough! If you are unable to stop the bullying with these methods, it may be time to enlist the help of the school or an authority. Separate yourself as much as possible from the bully and do not respond to his cruel actions.

If you are the parent or guardian of a child who's being bullied there are a number of things you can do to support your child and help him deal with the situation: The first step is to take the bullying seriously. It is not a natural rite of passage. If your child comes to you with reports of bullying, stay calm, be supportive, and let her know you are proud of her for talking to you about it. She is probably embarrassed and afraid of your reaction. Discuss with your child that bullying can happen to anyone and that he has done nothing to deserve it. Let him know it is the bully who is wrong and that you will work together to find a solution. Including your child in making a plan of action will both empower her and reduce her fear that you will make things worse for them by overstepping.

You should alert whoever is the authority figure where the bullying occurs; a bus driver, teacher, coach, or the like. If he is made aware of the bullying, he can keep a closer eye and perhaps step in when the bully takes action. If the bullying continues after a teacher or other authority figure has been alerted, you may want to ask for a meeting with the bully's parents. It is not a good idea to meet with them on your own. Instead, find out whether a guidance counselor or principal is able to act as a mediator. Educate yourself on the policies of the school regarding bullying as well as your local laws. If you feel your child's wellbeing is at stake, you may need to involve the law if the child's parents are unwilling or unable to help. I have a dear friend who lost her child from the actions of a bully and the parents of the bully were of no help, even after their child committed murder. So please, follow your gut instincts; if you feel you need to get the authorities involved, just do it.

Tell your child not to fight back. I know this is a tough one and will go against what most of us are taught, but it is really important. Fighting back may escalate the situation so that someone gets physically hurt. Instead, instruct your child to ignore the bully and walk away. I have done this personally, and it works wonders because the potential bully sees that he isn't getting under my skin and usually doesn't bother. At Sea World a number of years ago, a trainer for the orcas told the audience that there is only one way to discipline a killer whale. They are so large that any slap will feel like a tap, and when you yell at them, they just think it is praise. Essentially all reactions are seen as positive reinforcement for their behavior.

The only way to discipline a killer whale is to ignore it completely. When it realizes it is not getting attention, it will abandon the behavior and try another. Reward the behaviors you want to encourage with your attention, ignore them when they behave badly. If you react consistently they will learn to act in an acceptable manner.

Since that day I have thought of bullies as killer whales. Any time I want to try to put one in her place, to get into a war of words with her, I think of a killer whale and ignore her instead. Explaining this to your child may help them to remember in the heat of the moment to walk away from the bully.

Teach your child to avoid being alone in places where the bully could corner him. Use a bathroom the bully is not likely to be near, and find a friend and ask them to stick with you when you have to be around the bully. Tell your child it is okay for her to do the same for her friends, to stay with them when they are afraid of being bullied.

Help your child to develop a poker face. To have no reaction in the face of harassment is very difficult for anyone but especially for children who have less control over their emotions. They don't want to turn red or start crying in front of the bully, so teach them some techniques to redirect their attention. Teach them to count in their heads or practice a favorite song for them to sing in their heads when the bully talks so that instead of listening, they're focused on something else. If they get angry, teach them to write down angry words to release the anger without the bully knowing.

Have older children visualize themselves as an electrical outlet. Have them think of the bully as a toy monster. The monster cannot move or do anything without electricity. Every time your child reacts to the bully he should see it as allowing the monster to plug into his outlet and use his power against them. If instead she tells the bully to stop and doesn't react further, she is blocking the power source and the monster is deactivated.

Make sure your child knows that letting an adult know when bullying happens is not tattling or snitching, but the right thing to do. He may be helping other children as well as himself.

Luca's Story:

When I was being bullied at school, at first I wasn't going to report the incident. I thought the bullying was being directed only at me and that maybe it was somehow my fault. My mother explained to me that it wasn't "about me," it was about tolerance. It was about the bully feeling a need to threaten anyone who wasn't like him. My mother said that if he shamed me for being transgender, he might also shame someone who was African American, or who was fat, or any number of things. I thought about it and realized that I had heard him make fun of a Puerto Rican girl for her heritage. Realizing that reporting the bully might help other kids as well as me made me decide the right thing to do was to report him. Who knows? Maybe he would learn that what he was doing hurt people and then stop being a bully.

Encourage children to talk about the bullying with you, another adult, or their friends. Others may offer a solution your child did not think of, but more importantly, talking about the negative things said will remove their power. Your child will be less likely to obsess about and believe the awful things she is being told about herself if she can talk it out with someone else. Removing the isolation of bullying will most likely dampen or remove the long-term effects and the likelihood of self-harm or suicide.

Do not make your child feel as though all of your focus is on the bullying. This will solidify in the child's mind that it is deserving of all of their attention. Certainly discuss it but also ask about good parts of their day, things they are interested in and excited about. Give those things as much time and attention if not more.

Find ways to reinforce your child's self-esteem and help him to make friends. Get him into clubs, classes, or teams where he can do well and meet new children.

Excelling in a new area and learning that there are groups where she fits in can go a long way toward stopping the crushing self-doubt of victimhood. Many children find karate classes very helpful.

If your child is being cyber bullied anonymously, do your best to help her understand that she is not the problem, and that those who bully online are most likely kids without friends or interests of their own who feel the only way they can be part of things is to cause trouble. Reinforce with your child that trying to reason or argue with a cyber-bully is a waste of time because he has no interest in anything but upsetting people. Show her how to ignore these people. Make a bet with her that if she uses the ignoring technique, the bully will stop, and reward her for being strong enough to be the bigger person and walking away!

Ways to Make Your Life Bully Free

We cannot protect our children from everything bad that will happen to them but we can send them out into the world better prepared.

It is almost never too early to teach your children the self-confidence and empathy required to alleviate bullying. It is possible to begin with very young children. Assist children with understanding events and feelings as early as three years of age. At the end of their day ask them to tell you three good things that happened to them that day. This will help them distinguish the event and how it made them feel. Once they understand this, add a question about three good things that happened to someone else. This will increase their awareness of the moods and desires of others. It will be a positive introduction to empathy. Add questions about things they did that worked out well and things that did not go so well, and include the same question about others. This will introduce cause and effect to them so if bullying begins they will understand it is wrong. By helping them to separate action and emotion, positive and negative behavior and cause and effect, you will give them a head start such that if bullying begins, they will have a perspective and be less likely to blame themselves. Professionals and parents have found that when students begin school they are better able to understand and talk about bullying and their emotions when parents have had these conversations with them frequently as they have grown up.

Help your child develop a sense of who he is. Don't fall into the trap of believing you must reward his every behavior. He does not need a "participation trophy," or to feel good about himself every moment of the day. Instead, help your child know who she is and what she stands for. Let her know this is not dependent on how peers view her or feel about who she is. The issues her peers have are their own, and your child can remain true to her own ideals. Take the time to speak to your child, actively listen, and choose activities based on his interests and talents. Discuss his problems without dismissing them, and mention things that are unique about him or that may give them trouble.

Again, this is not about constant praise; it is about you showing her you know who she is and solidifying that for her, with the understanding that there is room for growth. When your child feels understood and understands himself, he will be less likely to bend to someone else's version of who he should be. he will become more of a leader instead of following others to fit in.

Also, by teaching empathy and understanding that everyone is an individual, you are reducing the risk of the child becoming a bully. Help your child to be a part of the solution and not just avoid the problem. You can do this by encouraging her to stand up for others and speak out against bullying. Let her know that by refusing to laugh along or be silent when one person picks on another, she takes away the power of the bully. Tell him about others, including yourself, who have done the right thing when it was most difficult.

Model the behavior you want to see your child display, this is key! If your child witnesses you reacting to a difficult or stressful situation in a calm and rational way on an everyday basis, she will mimic your reactions. She will see that being solution-oriented rather than flying off the handle is an option that works.

Also important is how you handle conflict within your home. If you or other adults in the home use intimidation techniques to get things done, you may inadvertently be teaching your child to bully. Instead of "because I said so," be prepared to explain your motivation to your kids for everything they question, because let's face it, kids question everything. Parenthood is a job, an obligation, and every moment is your opportunity to make your child the best person they can be, and the world a better place because they are here. You may just find you are becoming a better person yourself.

Explanations don't always have to be about why what it is you're asking for is better for the child. Let him know sometimes that what you are asking him to do—such as make his own bed or help set the table—is helping you and the rest of the family. There doesn't always have to be something in it for him. This will continue the lesson of empathy and working together toward a goal that may not be his own.

Encourage your child to have more than one circle of friends. Help her to get involved in after school or weekend programs that interest her. If she does happen to be bullied in one group, she will have other, separate groups of friends who will continue to value and support her. This will not only make her well-rounded but also be a boost for her individual self-esteem. She will recognize that the world is larger than one small group of people and that being an outsider in one group does not mean that she will always be an outsider to all groups.

Allow your child to become confident in his physical abilities. Some parents have difficulty letting their children be a part of physical activities because they do not want them to be hurt. Remember, kids *will* hurt themselves, no matter how hard you try to protect them! It will happen whether they are playing football or just running across the lawn. In fact, children who are involved in organized physical activities will be stronger and better able to protect themselves from injury. They will learn how to carry themselves in a confident way that bullies will recognize and ignore.

As mentioned in the last chapter, martial arts are a wonderful choice for teaching self-discipline, consequence, and respect; and will give them a better sense of self, while increasing their physical abilities. Defensive styles taught within most martial arts better prepare kids for peaceful and non-violent resolutions to conflict rather than falling back on a physical fight. Team sports are also a great way to teach kids the value of working together to achieve a common goal.

What to Do If Your Child Is the Bully

No one wants to believe their child is the one causing the chaos, but bullies do not just spontaneously show up. They are members of families—all types of families. They may be well behaved at home and you might find it difficult to believe your child would do this, but being defensive and not recognizing the problem will not help anyone. I like to call this scenario "the house angel and street devil"—sometimes kids can pull the wool over our eyes or we just don't want to see the reality of situations simply because we feel responsible. In most cases we should not blame ourselves; everyone has free will and sometimes it may be misguided.

It could be a matter of peer pressure, or one bad decision your child now feels locked into because of the reactions of others. It could be attention-seeking behavior or his reaction to not being able to make friends. Always remember, to kids, bad attention is perceived as better than no attention at all.

Whatever the reason the bullying began, you must address it with your child and she has to take responsibility for her actions, even if she was egged on by others. In the end, it was her decision to act.

When the first contact is made and someone tells you the difficult news about your child being a bully, listen calmly before you react. Try not to be defensive or emotional, but gather all of the information others have to offer. Let the person know you are taking what he has to say very seriously and that you will speak to your child. Go to your child and tell her what you were told without losing your temper. Ask her if there is any truth in what was said and give her an opportunity to tell the story from her perspective. Do what you can to find out what made your child make the decision to bully another person. Does she feel the need to take charge of others and control the group? Is she following the lead of another bully or doing it to get attention? Speak to her about whether someone treated her this way in the past. Determining the situation that started the bullying will lead you to ideas about how to help your child stop the behavior. Be clear with your child that her reason is important to share, but not by any means an excuse.

As a parent you must already realize that children will tell versions of the truth that may bend it to their favor. It is possible that when the account of the bullying is one child's word against another, you will never be able to determine with 100% accuracy who was at fault and what the complete truth is. That doesn't mean you should skip out on the consequences. When I was a kid, one of my brothers and I clashed and argued a lot because we were so similar in age and personalities. I recall the blame game never working with us—we both ended up in trouble with our parents whether it was my fault or his. After all, we had both participated in the fight.

Be clear with your child that no matter the circumstance, he is accountable for his own behavior. Make certain your child understands that he is doing real harm to his victim, and that this is not a joke, but a very serious offense. Perhaps you could sit with him and go over stories online of kids who were bullied, and ask him how he would feel if those things happened to him or someone he cares about; this is the best way to help him learn to put himself in someone else's shoes and to feel someone else's point of view.

Weigh the severity of the situation and make a decision about your child's consequences. If it is appropriate, get her to apologize. Before she apologizes, make certain she has a good understanding of what she did wrong, so that the apology is sincere. Beyond that, choose a punishment that makes sense for your child's age and interests. Grounding is okay for older kids but try to be more creative. Find out if there is a soup kitchen or another way for them to volunteer their time to increase someone else's quality of life. Help them to develop a sense of what is truly important in the world and how to serve their community; it is a great feeling knowing you are helping others and the earlier they learn this the better.

You may have to swallow your pride some, but work with the school and support the decisions they make for disciplining your child. This will reinforce to your child that bullying will not be tolerated and hopefully she will then be less likely to repeat the bullying.

Address the underlying issue. If your child is becoming a bully as a reaction to having been a bullying victim in the past, assist him with dealing with those emotions. If the problem is socially motivated, work toward healthier relationship skills. You get the idea; discipline without providing the child a different choice or outlet will only make your child more frustrated and confused.

Take this opportunity to get closer to your child, and to give her a healthy head start before she ends up traveling down a very negative road. You may want to consider whether your child would benefit from individual or family counseling.

Understand that every child goes through growing pains, gets hurt, and makes mistakes. Nothing about this makes you a bad parent, but how you react when these issues turn up will determine what type of parent you are and what sort of person your child will grow up to be.

Finding out whether your child is a cyber bully can be trickier, unless your child is bullying someone he knows in real life as well. There are some signs to watch for. Always talk to your kids about their interests; who are their celebrity crushes, what are their favorite shows, bands and sports figures? When they want to talk about these things, be available and interested. This way they will be less likely to classify your interest in what they do online as intrusive snooping. Listen for the way they talk about their experiences; are they excited about a new song or upcoming movie, or are they angry that some stupid person said something mean about their crush? If they seem to get agitated beyond a typical adolescent amount, it might be time to investigate their actions on the web more closely.

Shelley's Story:

We had our children sign "contracts" with us before they were allowed to go online. The contracts outlined the rules for going online, everything from never giving their name or address to someone online, to not engaging in bullying behavior. The contract stated that we—my husband and I—had to be given all passwords and had the right to look at the children's social media sites at any time. The kids complained but by the time they were teenagers, we had complete trust in them to police themselves, and whenever we were unsure, we could go in and check what they were posting on social media.

You may have noticed a unifying theme whether you are the parent of a bully or a victim: the better we know our children and instill a strong sense of self, empathy, and community; the fewer bullying issues we will all face.

Whether adult or child, one of the most important things we can all do is stand up against bullying whenever and wherever we see it. Standing by while someone else is victimized makes you a part of the bullying. Lead by your actions. Stand up speak out.

> **Bad attention is perceived as better than no attention at all.**

Bullying and LGBT+ Youth

Before I wrap up the first half of the book, Bullying at
School, I wanted to cover an important aspect that is
often missed or ignored. I strongly believe that it is of
merit to dedicate a chapter to this topic, as it is often
misunderstood by society. Since most people are attracted
to the opposite sex there is a disgust for or fear about
homosexuals instilled in many from an early age. This is
why people fear coming out, especially since they have
had to hear nasty words such as "fag" or "dyke" from
their family and friends since an early age. Harboring this
instilled homophobia creates internal conflict, low self-
esteem, and depression. It causes kids to stay closeted
and robs them of their happiness, and forces many to live
a lie. It is unintentional bullying from society since it is
embedded in our cultures, our families, politics, and even
some religions.

Homosexuality is not a disease and therefore it cannot
be cured, just as straight people cannot be changed to
gay. Once this is understood it is easier to rid ourselves of
homophobia, just as over time society is ridding itself
from foolish prejudices of other races and religions. Most
people are good by nature and sometimes when we have
fears of the unknown, we say things without thinking,
and unknowingly hurt someone we dearly love. It is so
important to make an effort to throw slanderous words

away, it may save a life. LGBT+ youth are much more likely to commit suicide than their straight friends. Have open discussions with your kids letting them know that you love them unconditionally. No one should be ashamed of who they are but should instead be proud, and keep in mind that sexuality is just a small part of who we are, it only shows to whom we are attracted. Our actions toward each other and how we treat ourselves are what we should be judged by.

Lesbian, gay, bisexual, and transgender (LGBT+) youth and those perceived as LGBT+ are highly susceptible to being bullied. Remember when we examined the suicide rates of bullied teens? Now compare that to the suicide rates for LGBT+ kids: The rate of suicide attempts for transgender youth is over 40%, the highest of any group of teens. LGBT+ youth are four times more likely, and questioning youth are three times more likely, to attempt suicide as their straight peers (thetrevorproject.org).

Luca's Story:

I'm a transgender boy. In the lunchroom, it came up that I use the boy's restroom. A boy who's a real jerk, "Dylan" stood up, pointed, and loudly made fun of me. He also said that I could be arrested for that, which isn't true! He said that I had no right to be in there and asked (loudly, so everyone heard!) if I still have "girl parts." First thing I did was to tell my mom. She suggested that I ask my guidance counselor hypothetically what the school would do if I reported the situation. I did, and my guidance counselor said that if I officially reported "Dylan," he would be brought in for questioning and a note would be made in his file, so if he ever discriminated against anyone for any reason—race, sexuality, gender, whatever—disciplinary action would be taken. I felt much better after reporting "Dylan" and talking to my guidance counselor and my mom.

Whether it is your kid or in your workplace, there are important considerations to address LGBT+ bullying.

Creating a Safe Environment for LGBT+ Youth: It is important to build a safe environment whether a person is straight or LGBT+; anyone can thrive if they are supported by their parents, schools, and communities, both physically and emotionally.

Support is critical: Building strong connections and keeping the communication lines open is critical for LGBT+ youth so that they do not feel rejected. It is important for them to know that there are people available for them to talk to if they need support and acceptance. It helps them to build confidence and fight bullies.

Schools play an important role to establish a safe environment. They can send a strong message that no one should be treated differently just because they are, or are perceived to be, LGBT+. Schools can add sexual orientation and gender identity protection to their school policies.

Schools can also create Gender/Sexuality Alliances (GSA's) to help create safe environments.
It is important to discuss bullying openly, both at school and at home.

Let your kids be who they are. If Johnny wants to play with dolls and do gymnastics, or Norma wants to take apart the lawn mower and rebuild it or play football, let them! Don't stop them from doing what they naturally love to do in hopes of protecting them, this will only instill self-doubts.

Last but not least, LGBT+ youth should be allowed to protect their privacy. Every person is unique and different, this is what makes the world interesting! If someone wants to keep their sexuality or gender-identity to themselves, let them. Don't push your hopes for them onto them; instead listen to their hopes and dreams, and help them to achieve them in their own way.

> *Homosexuality is not a disease and therefore it cannot be cured, just as straight people cannot be changed to gay.*

Part Two: Bullying at Work

Do You Have a Bully at Work?

When most of us envision a bully, we typically think about having trouble in the schoolyard or perhaps having a peer take one's lunch money. Although that certainly is one type of a bully, bullying is a problem that is by no means confined to school-aged children. As a matter of fact, there are many people who are bullied in the workplace, and they spend much of their adult life worrying about the same stresses that occur when children are bullied on the playground. If this is a problem for you, take heart, because there are solutions that can help to relieve the problem.

Although many of us may have felt as if we left bullying behind in our lives when we graduated from school, it is something that often follows us into our adult lives. The same children who at one time bullied us on the playground are also adults now and they bring their same tendencies along with them. The problem is, the bullying that takes place in the workplace affects us on a much broader level. Not only does it affect us emotionally and perhaps even physically, it can affect us financially and can hurt our family relationships as well.

In order to overcome the challenges presented by workplace bullying, you first need to identify the fact that you are indeed being bullied. Although it may seem obvious, the fact of the matter is that there are a number of signs that can easily point to the fact that you are dealing with the workplace bully. You will find that the chapter dealing with the signs of bullying is more than informative; it can help you in several areas of life.

One of the first things that many of us consider when we are being bullied at work is if it is possible to get the assistance of our superiors. That is, of course, if it is not our superiors who are bullying us. Although it may seem obvious that our bosses could help in such a situation, there are a number of reasons why his or her hands may be tied. In fact, you may find that you get the lowest response when you go to the top. We will discuss why that is the case and what you can do in order to get beyond it.

Perhaps you have considered some sort of legal solution to your problem, and it seems logical to think that there would be one available. In the following chapters, however, we are going to discuss the reason why a lawyer may not be able to assist you. Of course, there are sometimes legal solutions but you need to go into it with the right frame of mind, and you need to make the right decisions along the way. Unfortunately, there are also times when a legal solution will not present itself and we will examine why.

Learning about bullies and understanding some of the things that are not going to work can save you time and help you to get the matter cleared up as quickly as possible. Of course, this book will not stop with simply telling you why something won't work, I am going to tell you what works as well. As a matter of fact, there are a number of solutions that we will discuss in this book, any of which will work on its own, but they are very powerful when they are used properly together.

Here are a few suggestions I have found to work well that you may want to consider:

Confidence:

A bully will steal from you, even though they may not be stealing money. What they tend to take away from you, even when they are bullying you in the workplace, is your confidence. Unfortunately, the lack of confidence puts you in a position to be bullied even further, but there are solutions available. We will discuss how one of the top solutions is to build up your confidence, and I will give you the information necessary to do so effectively.

Avoid:

Another solution that we will discuss is how to take you out of the general line of fire that is being targeted by the bully. There are a number of ways to do this, some of which are relatively easy to implement, and others that are going to take a significant amount of effort on your part. When you are out of the line of fire of the bully, you often find that the solution presents itself and that you are no longer being bullied, simply because you are not where the bullying is occurring.

Mary's story:

Mary from Connecticut was dealing with a really tough older woman on her shift at a medium-sized manufacturing plant. Mary told me "I dealt with this woman for over a year, for some reason she hated me from day one. I loved my job but dreaded going in when she was working. I ended up gaining weight and even started getting grey hair. Everyone said she is just 'old fashioned and has an odd sense of humor;' well her humor was at my expense. Finally, I went to management and we decided that I change to another shift, which I was thrilled about because I can be home when the kids got off the bus, I never had to see her again and I dropped the weight I gained from stress within a month of the change!"

Make a Stand:

One other possible solution is to make a stand against the bully, and this is likely advice that you have heard for the majority of your life. Unfortunately, dealing with an adult bully who is harassing you in the workplace is much different, in many ways, than dealing with a bully on the playground. When you make a stand, you need to do it in a very specific way, and we will discuss how to do it in this book.

At times, you may be dealing with individuals in the workplace who are difficult to handle. This is also something that needs to be discussed, because it can cause many of the same problems that we might face if we are dealing with the workplace bully. If you are surrounded by individuals who are difficult to handle, it is important for you to learn some coping skills and how to handle the situation properly. In doing so, you will avoid many frustrating experiences that can harm you throughout your lifetime.

If there is one thing that is consistently a part of being bullied at work, it's the fact that you are going to have a significantly high stress level. Unfortunately, most of our stress levels seem to be off the chart even without having to deal with a bully, so the added stress of a bully can really push us over the edge. We will discuss some factors that will allow you to reduce the stress in your life, including some techniques that are used by first responders and other individuals who choose a lifestyle known to be very stressful.

It is important for you to handle the problem with a bully at work and to get beyond it. In doing so, you will put yourself in the position where you can live your life in a relatively calm and stress-free manner.

What is a Bully at Work?

It is important for you to take the proper steps so that you can deal successfully with your bully. It often requires that you start from square one, however, and that is often identifying the fact that you have a bully or perhaps even defining what a bully is in the first place. In this chapter, we are going to take a closer look at bullying, and help to define the parameters that could help you to know that you have a problem and that something needs to be done about it.

First of all, it's important to recognize that there are many different types of bullies. More than likely, we recognize that from when we were children, and we may have had a problem with bullying on the playground at that time. Bullying in the workplace goes even beyond our early ideas about bullying, because, while it may lead to all of the same problems that we have experienced in younger years, it now adds economic issues.

What does a bully do? The definition of a bully may differ from one place to another, but it essentially involves somebody harassing you in some way or another in a way that is causing you stress. Admittedly, there may be some difficult people at work, and we will discuss that further in this book, but bullies usually step outside of the lines. In addition, they usually target certain individuals, even though they may be somewhat jerks to everybody within the workplace. Perhaps you feel as if you are being targeted and experiencing one of the following problems:

Sabotage:

One of the ways that you may be bullied is that your bully may be sabotaging your ability to get work done. They may do this in a number of different ways, perhaps by interfering with your ability to work consistently and constructively, or they may even get additional work added to your assignment knowing that combined with your normal schedule it is impossible for you to get it complete.

Verbal Abuse:

Another common way that individuals are abused at work is verbally. It doesn't matter what your position is at work, or what position your bully happens to be in, there is no excuse for being verbally abused at any time. One of the reasons why the verbal abuse takes place is because the bully will want to put you in a position where you feel as if you are unable to fight back. By placing you in the lower position, they feel better about themselves. This is really important to remember; it was a lesson that took me years to actually sink in to my beliefs.

Intimidation:

Your bully may intimidate you in any number of different ways, including using humiliating tactics that will put you in a very uncomfortable situation. You may even find that you are threatened at work. You might have your ability to work at the location threatened or they may even threaten you physically. All of this is a type of abusive conduct and it is something that has no place in the workplace.

Physical Abuse:

If somebody in the workplace has abused you physically, bullying has certainly taken a huge step into a dangerous realm. As you will learn in this book, workplace bullying is often not illegal and there are many times when the company where you work will have their hands tied, simply because they don't have options for managing the situation. If any type of physical abuse takes place, however, there certainly is a legal case and it will help you to get the assistance that you need.

If you are being bullied in the workplace and you recognize that you have a legitimate cause for complaint, it is important for you to not feel as if you brought this problem on yourself. Being bullied is very difficult, and it can cause a level of mental stress that can even affect us physically. Unfortunately, the mental strain that often goes along with the bullying often makes us feel as if we are at fault for the problems we are experiencing. That is not the case and by working on your level of self-esteem, you can overcome this problem.

Another thing to keep in mind is the fact that you are not the only person that is being abused in the workplace. As a matter of fact, workplace bullying is a very serious issue and it occurs in almost any business where multiple people work. There is a certain degree of comfort that is felt when you understand that you are not alone in a difficult situation. That certainly is the case when it comes to workplace bullying.

Identifying the definition of a bully can help you to recognize that you are suffering from the difficulty in your place of employment. At this point, it is important to recognize the signs that you are being bullied and then to move on with the solutions that may present themselves, if you take certain steps. It is important that you know that you are not alone.

My Story:

I recall a time when I worked in a vending machine company and I dealt with one of the worst bullies I have ever met. He was passive aggressive, very nice to me face to face, but would torment me by moving machines in my path of work. When confronted he would just apologize and do it again. Finally, when I got the courage up to speak to the boss (who loved this bully) about the issue, he immediately started telling me stories of his past with bullies, from that day on I knew I was not alone and was able to take the steps to stop this bully whom I had to see every day. Within weeks he stopped and I was much happier during my work day.

What Are the Signs That You Are Being Bullied?

Most of us who deal with bullies in the workplace realize that we have a serious problem on our hands. The degree of difficulty that we face may differ from one individual to another, but there is no doubt that the trouble is there and that we need to do something about it for our own sake's and more than likely, for the sake of our families and friends. I personally am very aloof; I am usually so happy go lucky and so immersed in my own world that I don't even catch on when someone is trying to bully me, in fact, I call myself "dumb, fat and happy" when others ask why I didn't speak up about the situation. The truth of the matter is, I didn't even hear what the person was saying because I learned to block out negative or mean-spirited people at a young age.

It may also be that you feel as if you are being bullied at work but you are not really sure if it is a serious problem for you. After all, perhaps the problem is yours and not that of those around you. Understanding how to tell for sure that you have a problem is often the first step in the process of figuring out you're being bullied. In this chapter, we are going to discuss some of the primary signs that are seen both in and out of the workplace that make it obvious that you have a problem that needs to be dealt with now.

Often one of the easier ways for you to determine that you have a problem with the workplace bully is that you are having problems at work. Admittedly, the types of difficulties that you experience are going to differ from one situation to another but more than likely, you have experienced at least one of these problems and you may be experiencing many of them:

Anxiety:

One of the most common problems experienced at work when you are being bullied is that you will experience a heightened level of anxiety. Some people who have experienced this call it, "waiting for the other shoe to drop," as if there is always something bad just around the corner that is waiting to happen.

Work Is Never Good Enough:

Do you struggle to do anything at work that is accepted by your superiors? If you're being bullied by those who are in a superior position to you, they will likely give you a hard time about your work, regardless of how good it is or how hard you actually perform. In many cases, you will be thrown into the middle of a work situation without any prior time to prepare for it.

One Sided:

Do you feel as if you are always being harassed, yelled at or otherwise abused, and the abuser does not experience any type of backlash for doing it; but if you tried to stand up for yourself, you are severely reprimanded? This is often the sign of the workplace bully, this is common in both small family-owned businesses and in huge corporations—you feel as though favoritism is at play and thus, your dedication to the company will inherently drop, making you feel guilty for management's poor judgement.

Silent Support:

One of the problems that is fairly common among workplace bully situations is that all of your coworkers and perhaps even your superiors may admit that the workplace bully is out of line and has a personality that is very difficult to handle. If you asked them for some support to assist you in standing up to the bully, they will likely deny that they ever said anything about it.

Many of us who have to deal with the workplace bully have a very hard time keeping it contained within the workplace. Unfortunately, those of our friends and relatives on the home front may also experience the effects of bullying, simply because we bring our problems home with us. It often shows up in interactions with others, and we may see it in a number of different ways. The following are some signs of the common ways workplace bully shows up in our home:

Illness and Anxiety:

Many people who deal with a workplace bully experience a type of dread in the evenings and they may even feel as if they could become physically sick as a result of stress. The human body was made to stand up to a certain level of stress, but when we are dealing with a bully, our stress levels can easily overwhelm us and cause physical symptoms. Remember, stress is one of the leading causes of illness and overall deaths.

Obsessing:

Another common problem when you're dealing with a workplace bully is that you will constantly obsess about the situation or about work in general, I've done this on numerous occasions. You may recognize the fact that you are obsessing over work but more than likely, you will also be reminded of the fact that you are obsessing over a bullying situation as well.

Taking it out on others:

Unfortunately, the troubles that we face at work because of a bully will often spillover at home and we may find that we are taking out our frustrations on others. It is one thing to discuss a problem with your spouse, but it is quite another to take out your frustrations by yelling at him or her. In addition, children are completely innocent in this matter and should never be the victims of our frustrations.

Skewed View:

One of the problems that many people have when they are being bullied at work is that they begin to believe that it is their problem and that they did something in order to cause the difficulty. Quite honestly, workplace bullies look for an opportunity to bully others and they are the ones that are at fault, not you.

Advice:

Finally, you may hear from everybody that the best thing for you to do is to simply give up your job and to move on to greener pastures. You may hear this from everyone; including your wife, parents, children, doctor, and friends. In many cases, they may see something in you that you are unable to see yourself, and they may recognize that it is time for you to move on to another job and to leave your stressful life behind you.

These are just a few of the different signs that you may be experiencing if you are dealing with a bully in the workplace. Although there may be variations and each of us has our own individual problems, it is also likely that you are experiencing these problems as well. If you see them in yourself, it is likely that you are dealing with a workplace bully and that it is time to do something about it. This book will provide you with some answers to the questions that you may have.

It may seem simple, especially if you've been the victim of overt bullying, and you're probably wondering how in the world anyone could not know he was being bullied. Consider however, that bullying can be subtle at first, and perhaps there were signs it was going to begin before you realized it.

Adults may not be certain whether behavior they are experiencing in the home or workplace is bullying, or if they are merely being over-sensitive. Bullies are experts at making one question whether one is somehow responsible for the treatment one is receiving or whether one might be overreacting to something that isn't as serious as it feels. I have seen this firsthand; bullies are good at this.

In case you're still not sure if you're being bullied at work, here are some of the most common indicators:

• You are given a task or position for which you have no training or are not provided the time or the tools to perform well, and your results are constantly rejected by your boss without any constructive criticism.

• You are not allowed to complete tasks without outside interference.

• You are humiliated publicly with no consequences for those who attack you, but are immediately reprimanded for responding in a similar fashion.

• Others are told not to socialize, work with, or associate with you.

• The person who is upsetting you is undermining your social standing and the job you are hired to do.

• You are always worried or anxious, and expect bad things to happen.

• You feel sick the night before work, have trouble sleeping, and want to call out sick nearly every day.

• The only time you feel safe at work is when the person in question is not in the office or on the job.

• You talk endlessly about work problems at home.

• You develop high blood pressure and other health issues.

• When you are not at work you are exhausted.

• You lose interest in things you used to enjoy doing on your time off.

• You question whether you did something to set the bully off and find yourself second guessing your behavior and censoring yourself to avoid the involvement.

• You replay the incidents with the possible bully over and over obsessively in your mind.

• You are unable to concentrate and become forgetful, especially when it comes to short term information.

• When you report the issue to a supervisor or human resources, you are told they cannot intervene because it is not technically harassment. You are told this is something the two of you will have to settle on your own.

• Others agree with you privately that the behavior is not okay but will not admit to it in the presence of the bully for fear of becoming the next target.

• When you speak up and ask the person creating the problem to stop his behavior, he turns it around as if he is the victim, and says you are harassing him. He will also likely avoid eye contact with you and direct conversation, instead choosing to communicate via emails or other written media. Bullies for the most part do not deal well with direct confrontation. They do not want a light shined on their behavior.

My Story:

There was a woman where I worked who had a history of bullying people into quitting; she would brag that she did this for fun, but at the same time would always state she was right to push them to leaving because they did not do their job well. She would befriend someone and then seemingly for no reason turn on them. We sat near each other and spoke frequently, so I was friendly without joining in on her "mean girls" group. One day, completely out of the blue, she turned on me. She snapped at me and when I asked her what her problem with me was, in front of everyone she told me, "You don't want to go there with me." When I pressed and said I did, and that if she had something to say she should say it right then and there, in front of me instead of behind my back like she did with everyone else, she turned her whole body away from me and began to mutter that I was going to push her too far and she wasn't going to be able to keep her cool. This was her trying to turn the blame on me, to make me the bully and her the victim in front of our coworkers. I did not let it go. I told her I wasn't pushing anything, so she called me out and acted as if I had done something wrong, however,

I simply wanted to know what it was I had done to upset her, so that I could either explain myself or apologize. There was no reason for her to "lose it." She left me alone, and though I continued to wish her a good morning every day when we came in and told her to have a good day when we left, she did not speak to me for years. She also stopped bullying everyone and has not forced another coworker to quit. She has since gotten promoted to a job she enjoys more and we have become good friends. She no longer feels the need to place herself above her coworkers in a negative way because her hard work (and she had always been a hard worker) was being rewarded appropriately.

Adults are also bullied outside of the workplace. Rumor spreading, exclusion from group activities, and nasty comments can happen on sports teams, at the gym, at church, or any place adults interact on a regular basis. Bullying can even happen in the home. Roommates, spouses, friends of people who live in your home, adult siblings, and even parents of adult children can all use intimidation and all of the other tactics of a bully to make you miserable in the place that should be your safest refuge.

There is a stigma to being bullied as an adult that makes us less likely to tell others about our plight. We feel as though we should not be so easily manipulated or affected by the words and actions of others, and are embarrassed. This is only playing further into the bully's machinations. Find someone you trust and discuss it with them; you will feel better when you are not carrying the burden on your own.

> ***If you're being bullied by those who are in a superior position to you, they will likely give you a hard time about your work, regardless of how good it is or how hard you actually perform***

Why Your Boss May Not Be Able to Help

One of the first things that many of us may do if we are dealing with a workplace bully is to inform somebody in a higher position. Often, we will go directly to our supervisor in order to inform him or her that we have a problem with harassment or some type of abuse. Of course, we would expect that our supervisors would do something about the situation right away, but you might be surprised to learn that your boss is often not going to do anything about the situation. In fact, he or she may be one of the worst individuals to inform about your difficulty.

First of all, a supervisor in a larger company is going to be in a limited position to do anything about a workplace-bullying incident. The only option that they will likely have is to discuss the situation with others above them and they probably do not want to rock the boat for your problem. When you tell them about it, they may seem empathetic about your plight but it is unlikely that it is going to go any further than their office.

It may also be possible that your boss is going to view you as a troublemaker, even though you didn't do anything wrong. Unfortunately, he or she may simply give you the advice to ignore the situation, but as you likely already know, ignoring it is not always going to work to your advantage. If you find that this type of situation occurs, you may wish to ask for a transfer at that point if one is available.

Another reason why it may be difficult for a boss to handle a problem with the workplace bully is because of the same reason why we will discuss getting a lawyer can be difficult. Although bullying can be frustrating and it certainly can be the root of a very serious and stressful problem, it is not something that is typically defined as illegal. In fact, there is very little recourse available in order to control the problem and to correct it unless there is some type of physical abuse taking place or if it is a matter of racial or sexual harassment.

If you feel as if you have no place to turn other than to a boss, it is always best to choose somebody that is in the highest position possible, yet is still approachable. If somebody is going to be in a position to do something about the situation, it is going to be them. Of course, it can also have its own problems, because you may be viewed as a troublemaker by your direct superiors because you went over their head. It is a very touchy situation, and one that your need to approach with care.

In smaller family run companies it is best to go directly to the owner. If he is hands-on with daily tasks he or she will always have the best interest in mind for the company. Successful business owners know the importance of a smooth running company has to do with content employees who feel valued and appreciated. So most small business owners will try to nip the problem in the butt right away, in fear of losing a valuable and loyal employee, or for fear of hurting the reputation of the company, which the business owner feels is an extension of him or herself.

You might even try what "Luca" tried at school: Approach your boss first with a hypothetical, general situation—"If someone did this to me and I reported it to you, what action would you be likely to take?" Then you have valuable information to help you decide whether your boss can help you handle the bully in your workplace.

> *Successful business owners know the importance of a smooth running company has to do with content employees who feel valued and appreciated*

Why Lawyers May Not Be Able to Help

Another option that many people who are being bullied at work will consider at some point or another is trying to get legal assistance, and to overcome the problem in that way. This would seem somewhat logical, because it could hardly be illegal for an individual to cause such difficulty in the workplace. As you will learn, however, there are very few laws that govern workplace bullying, so in most cases it is possible for them to get away with it without any legal repercussions.

That doesn't mean, however, that there is never a chance for you to be able to deal with the workplace bully by means of obtaining a lawyer and getting the assistance. In fact, there may be specific reasons why you would consider doing so; we will discuss those reasons in this chapter as well. For now, let's talk about why a lawyer may not be able to help you with workplace bullying. Understanding this in advance can save you a lot of time and frustration; in some cases it can save you some money as well.

The first thing that you will discover if you were to talk to a lawyer is that there isn't a law in the United States that specifically addresses the problem of workplace bullying. In order for any type of legal action to gain ground and work in your favor, there has to be a law that is going to cover the situation. Of course, we are not dealing with a Wild West type of situation, where people are going to be able to do anything they want. At work, people must follow certain standards and although they may be able to get away with some bullying, they cannot get away with stepping over the line.

The unfortunate thing is, most bullies will not step over the line and do something that would cause them any type of legal difficulty. For example, if the bullying were to turn a bad corner and become physical, then you may be able to approach the situation from a legal standpoint. At that point, the problem is known as abuse and there are laws in the United States that make any type of physical abuse illegal. For common harassment, however, there is not much that can be done.

You also need to consider the cost involved in obtaining legal counsel to assist you with your problem. If you speak to an attorney and he or she feels there is some type of legal recourse that can be taken, the financial cost could end up being rather enormous. In addition, you may find that you are putting your job in jeopardy as a result of initiating legal action, and that can have some financial difficulties associated with it as well.

Finally, you are putting yourself in greater danger when you try to get the law involved, especially if there is not legal action that can be taken. Speaking with an attorney and making a public declaration can often end up in some type of retaliatory issue, and the bullying may even become worse. This is something you need to consider quite carefully, because you may be putting yourself at further risk for additional bullying and you will not get any relief as a result of speaking to a lawyer.

Chris's Story:

When I taught 5th grade in a local, urban school, my principal and I had had a couple of disagreements over discipline in the classroom. One afternoon, she announced over the loudspeaker that no students sent down by Mr. "Monroe" for disciplinary action would be accepted by the office. The class went wild, yelling, cursing, and throwing chairs and books, making me feel danger for myself and my more disciplined students. I was really shaken. After much thought, I decided that I'd been bullied by my principal and called a lawyer. The lawyer explained to me that without evidence, there wasn't much he could do. Even with real evidence, there was little he could do. He said he'd file charges if I wanted to go forward, but that he recommended against it, for the sake of my career. In the end, I was too afraid of repercussions to even go to my union rep. I went to a doctor, who wrote me a note about stress that allowed me to take all my sick days in a row, during which time I calmed down—and started looking for a new job!

Knowing all of this, you may consider your experience to be something that would have some legal ground, in which case you want to make sure that you are speaking to the right type of attorney. The best type of attorney to speak to in this type of case is one who understands employment law, rather than one who specializes in civil law. If you're going to have any type of legal footing when it comes to a workplace bully, it is often going to be from an employment standpoint but again, you need to weigh everything very carefully to determine if you are making the right move.

The only way that you are practically guaranteed to have a case against somebody who is bullying you in the workplace is if they are doing so in a discriminatory type of action. Most employment lawyers would jump on such a case and they would more than likely come out with you on top. Another reason to consider the possibility of legal action is if there was some type of physical abuse that took place. This is something that is always unacceptable, and it is illegal as well.

When hiring an attorney, consider the payment structure, because that is going to differ from one firm to another. If it is a case that is almost certain to be won, such as discrimination or physical abuse, the attorney may work on a contingency basis. She will plead your case and she will not charge you anything unless you win, and then she will take a certain percentage of the winnings. You can also have an attorney on retainer or you can pay the attorney an hourly fee, but each of those is going to cost you a considerable amount of money.

When you get right down to it, there is often nothing that can be done from a legal standpoint unless it is a matter of discrimination or physical abuse. Although bullying can be a very frustrating problem and it certainly can cause you a lot of emotional distress, the law is not on your side. You may still want to speak to an attorney about your particular situation, but if you do so, look for somebody that will hear your case without an upfront fee and don't let anyone, especially your bully, know that you are seeking legal counsel until you figure it all out and have a game plan.

Solution: Build up Your Courage

Up until this point of the book, we have discussed a number of factors that would help you to identify a workplace bully, and perhaps some things that you should not do when you are faced with such a problem. Beginning in this chapter, we are going to provide a number of solutions that may help you to deal successfully with the workplace bully and even to overcome the situation. Each of these solutions will work nicely as a separate tactic, but when you combine them, you may find that you are able to rise above the situation in the fastest way possible.

One of the first things that you should understand about the workplace bully is that he is lazy. Most bullies are not going to want to go out of their way to harass others, because that would make it difficult for them. More than likely, you are somebody that has a rather kind demeanor or you may find it difficult to stand up for yourself in stressful situations. Like a lion that looks for the weaker members of the herd before deciding which one to attack, a workplace bully has chosen you as a target.

Of course, you should never consider the possibility that you are somebody who deserves to be bullied in any way. Unfortunately, it is often kind individuals or those who are relatively mild who face this type of problem, and there is certainly nothing wrong with that type of personality. If you find that it is causing you difficulties with being bullied in the workplace, you may need to take control of the situation by taking a step that might be outside of your comfort zone. It involves building up your confidence and standing up for yourself, which may be something that is difficult for you.

My Story:

For years I just ignored people who taunted and bullied me, I figured it was best to just walk away and keep the peace. I knew I was targeted because I was the "nice guy" or the "happy go lucky guy" and figured it would just go away. Finally, after realizing people were targeting me since I was easy-going and kept to myself, I stood up for myself. In a serious tone in front of the rest of my co-workers, I made it known that I was fed up with one bully's nonsense, and that he should take a good hard look at his own insecurities about himself and work on them instead of pushing them off on others. I knew he was insecure about his weight issues and alcohol abuse, and this is why he projected them onto me, hoping it would take the focus off of himself. Looking at a bully's motives will always help you to understand why they are bullying others, which in turn will help you to find the correct solutions to stopping it.

Understanding Our Level of Self-Esteem:

Although there are many things that take place in our lives that can lead to difficulty with low self-esteem, it is often a problem that starts in our childhood. Because of the experiences we have when we are young, it is thought that our self-esteem develops during that time and it can either be one that is relatively high or relatively low. If we have low self-esteem, we are more than likely to be a victim of workplace bullying, but there are things that can be done to build your confidence.

The fact that you are feeling low self-esteem could display itself at a very young age with bullies as well. It has been noted that individuals who dealt with a bully in their younger years may also have a problem with a similar situation in their older years at the workplace. The reason this is the case is because the personalities are generally the same, it is just the dynamics of the situation have changed. Your bully at work was likely a bully at school, and if you are being bullied, it is likely that you were bullied at a younger age as well.

Understanding How to Manage Conflict:

You also need to consider that standing up to a bully or at the very least, managing the situation, is often going to involve a level of conflict. This may be something that is outside of your comfort zone but if you work on it, you will find that you are able to manage conflict with the least amount of problems possible.

In part, it is your mindset that is going to be a roadblock in dealing with conflict in your life. You may feel as if any sort of conflict is bad and that it is always going to have a negative consequence for you when it occurs. The fact of the matter is, however, a degree of conflict may be necessary for normal human interaction, and when you're dealing with somebody that is out of line, such as a workplace bully, the need for conflict may even be stronger. When you understand how to manage conflict and to resolve the situation, the ball may actually be in your court.

There are also differences in types of conflict, some being destructive and others being constructive. There is nothing wrong with you disagreeing with somebody at work, especially somebody who is bullying you in some way or another. Being able to put up a healthy debate on the subject and perhaps even challenging him at the same time may be enough to get him to back down.

One of the worst things that you can do, however, is to ignore the problem that you are facing. As a result of low self-esteem and a desire to resolve conflict properly, many individuals simply bury their heads in the sand and do nothing about the situation. This can be disastrous, because you are providing a greater opportunity for the bully to attack.

You can also learn some type of conflict resolution that can help you to deal with the situation in the best manner possible. In many cases, it involves remaining calm in a difficult situation and being forthcoming with what is bothering you about what the bully is doing. In addition, you need to be able to listen to the bully if he is willing to speak about the situation calmly and then work with him to come up with some type of solution that is going to work for everyone involved.

Building up your courage can take time and effort, but it will also provide you with the ability to do something about the problem that you are facing. Remember, you are not building up your courage in order to overpower the bully, you are building it up to the extent where you can stand up for yourself in crisis.

Always remember "we all wipe our butts the same way," meaning, we are all the same; no one is better than anyone else, don't ever let anyone lead you to believe any differently.

> *For years I just ignored people who taunted and bullied me, I figured it was best to just walk away and keep the peace.*

Solution: Take Yourself out of the Line of Fire

Something that you should know about bullies in the workplace—or in any situation for that matter—is that bullies are opportunists. In order for bullies to harass somebody, they need to have the opportunity to do so and they are looking for the path of least resistance. If you find yourself in a situation where you are the target of a workplace bully, sometimes you can simply remove yourself from the situation. There are a few opportunities for you to do so and more than likely, one will work for you. I know that these suggestions will be tough, but in some cases they are needed.

Move Your Physical Location:

Sometimes you find that you are dealing with a bully who works in close proximity to you on a daily basis. Perhaps he has a cubicle that is adjacent to yours and you are simply an easy opportunity for him to flex his bully muscles. One of the options that you may have available is to move your physical location, thereby taking yourself out of the line of fire directly.

Of course, in order for you to make such a move in the workplace, you are often going to have to have permission from your boss. Discussing the situation with the boss is not always the best thing to do, as we discussed previously. It may eventually become necessary, but at this point, simply tell your boss that you would like to move your office for other reasons, including being more productive. He or she will likely agree to such a move.

Change Your Circumstances:

Another way that you may be able to avoid a problem with the workplace bully is to change your circumstances. Perhaps you have to work with the bully on a specific project on a daily basis, and that may be contributing to the problem that you are experiencing. If there are other options that would put you on a different team or perhaps even in a different department, it may be to your advantage to make the move.

Change Your Shift:

If you want to stay with the same company but you cannot manage the harassment from your bully, it may be possible to switch shifts to get out from underneath the situation. Of course, in order for you to do this, you need to work for a company that runs multiple shifts, but if it is an option, it may be something that you want to consider.

Change Your Job:

When you have tried practically everything that is possible and you are still dealing with a problem with the workplace bully, it may be time to consider changing jobs. This should be the last thing considered, because it can be very stressful and you may even find yourself in a difficult situation if you're unable to find other employment. However, beginning a search for another job may give you a sense of empowerment that will help you to deal with your bully, whether you actually leave your current job or not.

When all of your other options are exhausted, including waiting things out and moving within the same company, quitting your job may seem like a viable solution. You need to consider the possibility, however, that you are just going to move from one bad situation into another, because there are workplace bullies in almost every type of environment. If you have the personality that allows others to bully you easily, they will seek out the opportunity to do so once you are on their turf.

That is why it may be to your advantage to work on yourself and to build up your self-esteem before you move to another company. In doing so, you will be more likely to face any type of workplace bullying successfully when it occurs in the future and you may even find that you are able to manage what is taking place in your current job as well. What I do is read up on the subject, as you are doing now. This seems to help remind me that there are others who have dealt with bullies successfully.

Another great way to help build self-esteem is simple exercising every day. I make it a habit to constantly work out, walk, or ride my bike for at least 30 minutes a day, getting outside and breathing in the fresh air, or going to the gym and joining others who are getting healthier seems to build my self-esteem and self-worth instantly.

Setting goals and surrounding yourself with upbeat people will always help to resolve almost any issue which comes your way, even workplace bullies.

> *Perhaps he has a cubicle that is adjacent to yours and you are simply an easy opportunity for him to flex his bully muscles.*

Solution: Standing Up for Yourself

As you have likely recognized by this point in the book, there are a number of different ways for you to effectively manage a problem with a bully. In this chapter, I am going to provide you with another solution that can be used in almost any type of bullying situation: Standing up for yourself. There is nothing wrong with doing so and it does not need to be an overly aggressive action. By simply standing up for your rights, you may prevent the problem with bullying from continuing to happen in a number of ways.

The first step in this process is to set specific limits on what is acceptable behavior and to make it well known. This is called "setting boundaries" and you can think of it like building a fence around your property. Not necessarily a high, blockade fence. Maybe it is just a small, picket fence. What's important is that just as a fence will keep the neighbor's dog from urinating on your petunias, setting limits of acceptable behavior for yourself might help you stop your colleague from continuing to bully you.

For example, you may be dealing with the problem with harassment, and if it is ongoing, it can cause you mental stress and can affect your quality of life. Identifying the type of harassment that is taking place and letting the bully know that you will no longer put up with it is should be one of your first steps in standing up for yourself. It can be difficult to do, but the effect of doing it is well worth the effort.

Along with letting the bully know how far things have gone, it is also a good idea for you to let him or her know how it is impacting you. For example, you may state that you are not going to accept being yelled at any longer at work because it is affecting you and your performance at work, as well as having an effect on your home life, and that is completely unacceptable. As long as you spell things out specifically to the bully, it is likely that he or she will get the picture.

Finally, don't leave it at just letting the bully know what is wrong and how it is affecting you; let him know what he can do differently. For example, he may verbally abuse you because he feels you are not working quickly enough, and that is unacceptable behavior. You can let him know, however, that there is nothing wrong with him letting you know that he would like you to work faster, but you would not accept the abuse at any further point.

Once you have set these guidelines in place, it is important for you to stick with anything that you have stated. If you simply state your intentions and allow the bully to return to his behavior without any repercussions, it is unlikely that you are going to see any benefit from your effort. On the other hand, continuing to point out the unacceptable behavior when it does occur may eventually produce the desired results.

Telling the bully about his behavior is one way of confronting him, and it certainly can be a difficult situation to be in. It is quite a different thing, however, to give him "a taste of his own medicine," provided it is appropriate behavior on your part.

"Carla's" Story:

I once knew somebody that was dealing with a boss who was somewhat of a hothead. She called him on the telephone to let him know that she was running late for work, and the boss exploded—yelling continually for several minutes without taking a breath. Suddenly, it dawned on "Carla" that she was actually at fault for the situation. After all, she had control of it because she was holding the phone to her ear, and the abuse was coming through that channel. She took action and simply hung up the phone, figuring that she would handle the situation when she was standing in front of the boss. As it turned out, the boss was somewhat impressed by the fact that she took that action, and the few minutes that it took her to get the rest of the way to work was enough to allow the situation to cool off. A rule I implemented at work is if you are in a bad mood and I call, let it go to voice mail; it is simply rude to pick up the phone with a nasty demeanor, instead, call me later when you aren't stressed!

Have you ever considered the fact that you may not be the only person that is being bullied at work? In some cases, you may be so wrapped up in your own situation and the stress that it is producing that you may not recognize that other individuals are in a similar situation. As they say, there is safety in numbers and if several of you are being bullied at the same time, you may find the mental strength to stand up to the bully when you take your stand together.

Of course, you will want to have a solid game plan in place before you try this, but it is one that can be very effective. When there are multiple people telling a bully that the conduct is unacceptable, it can really have an impact. More than likely, the bully will no longer feel confident in his ability to continue to get away with his behavior and he may seek greener pastures.

Finally, there may be no other choice but to talk to management or to the HR department about the situation. Although earlier in this book we discussed the possibility that it could be problematic to do so, it may sometimes be the best choice available. It really depends upon the circumstances, but if you are going to talk to the boss, you'd better make sure that you are backing up everything that you say with facts and evidence.

Rather than just going to the boss blindly to discuss the situation, document everything that you possibly can about the situation before you go into the meeting. Have specific dates, actions, and reactions written down so that you can spell them out to your boss, and let him or her know that you mean business. Even if your supervisor is not accustomed to getting involved in such situations, it may be possible that he or she will get involved when he or she sees how serious you are about it.

Standing up for yourself may be outside of your comfort zone, especially if you're dealing with low self-esteem or if you are simply a mild individual, like me. It may also be that you have a skewed sense of standing up for yourself, thinking that you need to be ultra-aggressive and to win, rather than to come to an agreement. The fact of the matter is, if you understand how to handle conflict and you are able to stand up for yourself in a calm and dignified manner, it can go a long way in helping to put the fire out in the situation. In the 19 years I have spent at a company in a management position I have never, not even once, needed to raise my voice or yell at anyone. I firmly believe you are much better off staying calm in every situation, walking away from the stressful situation for a moment, and always standing up for yourself and your beliefs in a respectful way; this will always work better than a shouting match where no one wins. You don't have to join in every fight you're invited to!

> *As long as you spell things out specifically to the bully, it is likely that he or she will get the picture.*

When People Are Difficult to Handle

Up until this point in the book, we have been dealing specifically with workplace bullies and the problems that they can cause. At this point, we are going to shift gears to a certain extent and talk about dealing with individuals who may be difficult, but are not necessarily bullies. In either case, it can cause a lot of stress for you, but if you handle the situation properly, you will be surprised with how far you are able to take things.

First of all, you need to determine if the individual is someone everybody considers to be difficult, or if the difficulty is directly between the two of you. You will likely find that the situation is much more easily resolved when there is more than one individual involved. If he or she is being difficult to you but not to anyone else, you may be actually dealing with a bully and not somebody who is just difficult to manage.

Before we discuss any possibilities for handling the situation, it's important to mention that you should never lose your professionalism. If you take some type of retaliatory response, doing something that may be considered childish just to make yourself feel better, you may be putting your own job at jeopardy. Continue to deal with the individual professionally, even if he or she makes it difficult for you to do so from time to time. To do less is a recipe for disaster!

You may find there are many similarities to dealing with a difficult person and dealing with somebody who is a bully. In most cases, it involves confronting the individual in some way or another, perhaps even standing up to him and any improper behavior that he may be exhibiting. Most individuals who are aggressive will not remain so if they are not able to stand up for themselves on solid ground. Anytime you are able to get on even ground with a bully, it is likely that a solution will present itself.

At times, it may be necessary for you to simply take your leave of the situation. This can be a difficult thing, especially if you're in the middle of a meeting or if the two of you work in close connection with each other throughout the day. You may find that, from time to time, getting up and walking away to get a drink of water, or simply to cool off in another location is the best option available. It may be just what is necessary to allow the other person to cool off as well and to let the situation settle itself. It is important to recognize that the type of difficulty that you may be facing with somebody at work is going to vary greatly from one situation to another.

As an example, one of the reasons why it may be difficult to work with somebody is because they have a problem with halitosis (bad breath). This is a situation that can be difficult, but you need to avoid doing something childish, such as anonymously putting some Lifesavers on their desk. Simply telling them, gently, that they have bad breath will often solve the situation. After all, they may be unaware that they have a problem. A similar solution is possible in many other, more difficult cases. I always make it a point to let coworkers, friends, family, and even clients know when there is something caught in their teeth or they have a snot hanging from their nose, and they almost always appreciate that I said something because they know I am doing it out of respect and love—I know I appreciate it when someone tells me that I have BBQ sauce on my chin or my zipper is down, otherwise I would probably go through a good portion of my day before realizing it!

You should also consider the order of operations when you are confronting any type of the situation with a difficult co-employee. Even if they annoy you to the point where you can hardly stand it, you should not retaliate directly or try to solve the situation by going over their head. The first step is that you should talk to the person directly and in a private manner. You may find that the problem is able to be resolved quickly when no one else is involved.

If you take the initial step and do not see any benefit from doing so, don't be too quick to blow the whistle and try to go over their head. In addition, try to keep any talk at your workplace to a minimum when it comes to the problem that you are experiencing. Other people are likely to discuss the problem, and it may get blown out of proportion. If you don't see any benefit from taking the initial step, simply talk to the offender again and see if it can be resolved. It may be possible that overcoming the problem is as difficult for them as it is for you.

If the situation continues to be a problem and it is not easily resolved, it may be time for you to get somebody else involved. In this instance, speaking to a superior or to a neutral party may be the best option available. In doing so, you may be moving forward to a solution rather than allowing the problem to escalate because you did not handle it appropriately.

Stress Busters to Relieve the Strain

If there is one thing that is consistent among those dealing with the workplace bully, it's the fact that they are under a considerable amount of stress. Our bodies were made to handle a certain amount of stress, and it can even be beneficial, when it is applied properly. Unfortunately, many of us are dealing with stress to the extent where we are unable to handle it, and it may even be considered a chronic problem. Rather than considering this to be part of life, you can actually do something about it.

In this chapter, we are going to discuss some techniques that I use for overcoming stress that you will want to consider. When you put these suggestions into practice, it can really help to reduce your stress levels, and may help you from a physical and a mental standpoint. After all, stress often affects us in that way, so it is something for you to consider carefully.

Pay Attention to Your Health:

More than likely, you are aware of the fact that our physical health is closely associated with our mental health. That is why taking care of your physical health can make a difference in how you feel and handle a stressful situation. In this section, we are going to talk about a few ways that you can manage your physical health and see positive results in your stress levels.

Limit Your Sugar Intake:

One of the problems that many people face with their diet is that they tend to focus on a lot of sugar. We may enjoy eating sugary snacks and high carbohydrate foods that are quickly digested, providing a massive amount of glucose to the bloodstream. When your blood sugar level is off, you may feel a number of different symptoms but it is going to cause problems in most cases. By reducing your sugar intake, you can often reduce your stress. When I stopped drinking alcohol and soda I almost immediately dropped 15 pounds, and my stress levels dropped immediately. If you give up just one thing and substitute it with something good (I joined a gym and started exercising daily), you will be on the right path toward a happier and less stressful life.

The easiest way to do it is to avoid any type of refined sugar when possible. Of course, most of us will reach for a snack cake when we are stressed out, but you need to try to overcome that urge. In addition, focus on foods that are lower on the glycine index, because they provide a more stable level of sugar to the bloodstream. You don't need to choose only foods that are low on the glycemic index, but try to strike a balance.

Exercise:

There are benefits to exercise that will reduce your stress significantly. One of the reasons why exercise can help with stress is because it releases chemicals in the body that are known as endorphins. These endorphins produce a natural high and can make you feel good, something that will last you throughout the day. Many people who are under a lot of stress try to exercise daily, and it really seems to help.

Another reason why exercise can help with your stress is because it has beneficial effects on your body-image. You may find that you are losing weight and putting on some healthy lean muscle, and when you feel good about yourself in that way, it will reduce your stress. In addition, exercising may provide a level of self-confidence that will help you to overcome the workplace bully directly. As a forty year-old guy who has never lifted weights or done cardio daily until two years ago, I feel healthier and happier than I did when I was 25 years old. Exercise is now part of my lifestyle and I no longer consider it a chore. This can be one of the keys to eliminating stress in your life too.

Hydration:

One of the easiest ways for you to improve your health is by keeping yourself hydrated. Most people will do quite nicely on three liters of water daily, but you may want to drink a gallon or more if you exercise regularly or if the weather is hot outside. In addition, doing a daily kidney flush, in which you drink a full quart of water within ten minutes of waking in the morning may have a positive effect on your mental outlook throughout the day.

A Deep Breathing Exercise That Works:

You may have heard of various breathing exercises that are supposed to help with stress but not all of them work as well as others. Although it is important for you to pay attention to your breathing and stress can certainly have an effect on your breathing, simply breathing more deeply is not necessarily going to have the effect that you want. The following exercise, however, has been proven to help reduce stress because it balances the carbon dioxide and oxygen levels quickly and effectively. It is even an exercise that is taught to first responders to deal with stressful situations.

The breathing exercise is called Square Breathing, and you should try to do it standing still or in a seated position. It is also possible to do it while you are walking, but you do run the risk of hyperventilating. It involves a four-step breathing process, and each individual step is done to the count of four. Keep your count slow and steady, and don't speed up the counting through any part of the process. If it becomes difficult to maintain holding your breath to the count of four, you can drop your count to three but keep it consistent.

Step One: Breathe In—The first step in the Square breathing process is to breath in. You want to take a deep breath but you don't want to fill your lungs to the point where it is uncomfortable. You would begin with your lungs comfortably empty and breathe in through your nose, allowing your lungs to fill completely and making sure that you are also properly engaging the diaphragm.

Step Two: Hold Your Breath—Now that your lungs are comfortably full, you will want to hold your breath to the count of four. Some people may struggle to hold their breath because they have a problem, such as asthma or COPD. If you find that it is difficult to hold your breath comfortably, you can reduce the count to three but make sure that you maintain that same count throughout the entire process. Eventually, you will get used to the sensation of holding your breath.

Step Three: Breathe Out—The next step in the process is to breathe out through your open mouth. This step is also done to the count of four, and you should not breathe out to the point where you are forcibly expelling the air from your lungs. It should be a comfortable process; after all, we are trying to relax.

Step Four: Hold Your Breath—The final step in the Square breathing process is to hold your breath. You will hold it to the count of four and if you experience any discomfort or anxiety, you can reduce your count to three. The entire Square breathing process should focus on your overall comfort.

The four-step process is considered one single exercise, but you can repeat that breath four times, running through the same process each time. The overall process does not typically take any longer than a minute, but the effects of doing it can be profound. You may find that you are running to the Square Breathing process to help keep yourself calm at work, at home, or even when you are under stress while driving.

Another key to stress is to "detach" every day. You should consider detaching from the electronic world for at least ten minutes every day. In recent years, we have become so accustomed to our cell phones, tablets, and computers that we rarely ever have a moment where we are not checking them. In fact, it is estimated that the average smartphone user checks his or her smartphone at least once every six minutes. In order to overcome this problem, we need to do more than trying to set our cell phone down from time to time; we need to make it a part of our life.

Some people refer to this as a daily detachment but regardless of what you call it, it is a way for you to get back in touch with yourself and to leave the electronic world behind. Quite simply, it involves turning off your cell phone, your tablet, your computer, and any other electronic device that would interrupt you during the few minutes that you take part in this exercise. During this time, you will not be receiving any emails, text messages, or updates to your Facebook status.

Some people find it to be terribly difficult to be without their electronic devices, even for a short amount of time. The fact that it is difficult shows us how much of a habit it is and how much it is affecting us on a very personal level. When you combine the stress of always being available and feeling as if you have to answer every message that comes your way within a matter of seconds with the stress of dealing with a workplace bully, it can truly get overwhelming. Simply giving yourself a few minutes to reset every day and shutting down during that time may make a huge difference, allowing you to reduce your stress and to see how to deal with your bullying situation successfully. I turn my phone off at least three hours a day! The key is to just let your family and friends know that you may take a while to get back to them, and most will not be upset—heck, you may even start a healthy trend among your friends and family!

> *Our bodies were made to handle a certain amount of stress, and it can even be beneficial, when it is applied properly.*

Final Words

Bullying is not something that can be explained by a simple dictionary definition. In fact, textbook definitions and the popular media tend to perpetuate stereotypes about bullies and bullying in general. It is important to abolish any ideas that you have about bullying, and then to adopt my approach and your own research to define it, keeping an open mind that bullying is just a challenge. You have faced many other challenges in your life and you can handle the bullying challenge as well.
In the book, I have tried to cover recognizing signs of when you or your child may be being bullied, in both offline and online scenarios.

By giving examples from people just like you and me, I have hopefully helped to dispel any hurdles to understanding why bullying unfairly happens to one child over another. While bullies may exist for a number of reasons based on their home environment, being subject to being bullied themselves, or through a particular social context, it can be difficult to discern the absolute reason why a bully in your area does bully. What I hope I have clarified in this book is why bullies may bully your child in particular. By demonstrating this through various scenarios, I have given you the tuition you need to support a solution-oriented approach.

As the book progressed into action, it focused on a mindset that should be developed when approaching difficulties. The specific methods varied depending on the situations, however, I stressed the importance of being rational and prudent, deterring actions that may worsen the bullying situation. Prudence is important because in many situations, the fastest solution is not always the best

I have provided you with the key points on how to effectively beat bullying and how to step up, to take all of your knowledge and put it into action. The methods suggested in the book are designed to not only give you the mental tools to approach the information that you have read in the latter portions of the book, but also to motivate you and encourage a mindset towards initiative. When you are motivated to achieve something, it motivates others to follow you. Many companies employ managers who are dedicated and passionate about achieving goals. These managers are paid high wages with the key responsibility of motivating others by their example. While the context is different, the concept remains the same.

This book has been presented like a challenge because a challenge begs to be overcome by a person who is ambitious enough to take it on. Overcoming bullying can make a person more self-confident, persistent, and resilient than his or her peers in adulthood. Without solving a bullying situation, a person can become just the opposite.

This creates enormous incentive to gather the motivation necessary to conquer the challenges at the present as well as the ones that lie ahead. By reading this book and implementing its techniques, you are working to change your child's present and future as well as setting an example for other parents around the world! Just take a moment to think what a great thing you can do for our society! When you deal with someone who is bullying you—for example, in the workplace—you demonstrate behavior and techniques that will help your children to grow into healthy, self-assured adults.

Remember that no matter what happens during your journey in overcoming, you will inevitably face difficulty, so do not expect an easy path. However, if something is too easily obtained, it is probably of little worth. The benefits of beating bullying are far greater than the investment of time put into it and never forget the fact that wounded people make the best healers. Use those wounds as strengths not excuses.

Resources

Here is a brief list of websites that I recommend you checking out, these are by far my favorite among the many that I researched in the making of this book.

School bullying:

www.teenviolencestatistics.com

www.stopbullying.gov/kids

www.bullyingstatistic.org

www.nces.ed.gov

www.pacerkidsagainstbullying.org (great site to get your kids on – very interactive)

www.nobullying.com/bullying-suicide-statistics/

Workplace bullying:

www.workplacebullying.org

www.bullyingstatistics.org (great workplace section as well as schools)

www.nobullying.com

www.brandongaille.com/24-important-statistics-of-bullying-in-the-workplace/

www.americanspcc.org

Acknowledgments

I am grateful to all of the people who took the time to email, call, or meet with me to discuss their personal stories; all of which are included in the book. I know it was not easy and took courage, but your contributions have helped me and I am certain will help all who read them.

Thanks to Shelley Stoehr for editing this book. I gained so much from Shelley's suggestions, knowledge, and encouragement; which stimulated my thoughts through numerous drafts. Shelley's expertise and experience brought this book to life. I highly recommend Shelley Stoehr to anyone who is looking for an editor; be sure to get her information in the back of the book in the section "About the Editor" and check out her books, sites, and pages; she is an amazing writer!

I owe a great deal of gratitude to Vipul Sachdeva for helping in the research of the topics of bullying. Vipul spent many hours finding facts and contributed significantly to my perspective of bullying.

Thanks to my brother Jack Keller for all of his input and medical expertise on the subjects of bullying. His long talks on the subject taught me to follow my sixth sense, my "gut instinct" on all matters. As Jack would tell you, a lot of people in the medical field chose the medical field because wounded people make the best healers. Jack has helped me in all three of my published books and I appreciate him more than he will ever know!

Thanks to Chris Nastu, Sr. for allowing me to add his heartfelt poem to this book about being bullied growing up. You can find Chris's poems at www.allpoetry.com/cnastu

I would like to give special thanks to all of my family and friends for being a big part of my life and inspiring me to pass along some of the positive messages that they have woven into my life every day. You know who you are and I love you!

Thank You Note to You, My Readers

Thank You, readers! I am so grateful to all of you who make it possible for me to follow my dreams of doing my part in helping our world to be a better place, by planting a few seeds of love and encouragement into the lives of my readers. I am blessed to be able to share my experiences with you and encourage you to follow your dreams, no matter how difficult it may seem to achieve at this moment. Together we can improve our communities with our combined skills, knowledge, hard work, and passion.

Thank You for picking up my books, reading them, and for all the reviews! It humbles me every time I read a new review, see new comments on my websites, get new followers on Facebook, and when I personally meet each of you at book signings and readings. To find out when I will be in your area doing a signing or speech, sign up to my Facebook page: Life In A Week...A Book About Being Really Happy, and my websites: www.bulliesamongus.com and www.lifeinaweek.com. If you have not left a review on Amazon.com please do so when you have a moment, I sincerely appreciate them all, as they help me to continue to share my message with others.

Again thank you for being so passionate about my books and audios, and for wanting to connect with me; I look forward to hearing from you!

About the Author

Michael Shawn Keller was born and raised in a small city in Connecticut with five brothers and two sisters, he has always enjoyed helping others to smile and to simply enjoy each day. Michael started working at a very young age and believes that we all should learn something new each day whether we are two or ninety-two. He enjoys reading, writing, working, traveling, camping, and simply being around his family and friends, laughing.

Michael helps to manage a small, family-run business during the day; and researches and interviews people part-time in the evenings for the subjects of his books. Each book is on topics that he feels are truly important and he hopes to encourage others to write about their stories—
together we can learn and grow from each other, while having a few hearty laughs along the way!

Michael has written two other books: "Life in a Week" A Book About Being Really Happy and "Life in a Week" What is Spirituality, both of which can be found online at Amazon, Barnes and Nobles, Books A Million or at Michael's websites, www.lifeinaweek.com or www.bulliesamongus.com.

About the Editor

Shelley Stoehr is a writer (mostly edgy, Young Adult fiction), and a freelance ghost writer and editor. Her books include *Crosses, Weird on the Outside, Tomorrow Wendy,* and *Saving Bone*. She is the co-author of *Weresisters.* Shelley lives in Connecticut with her husband, two children, a dog, three cats, a rat, and two fish. Her website is www.shelleystoehr.com.